The Other Side Of Love

The Other Side Of Love

HANDLING ANGER IN A GODLY WAY

GARY CHAPMAN

MOODY PRESS

CHICAGO

ISBN: 0-8024-6777-6

3 5 7 9 10 8 6 4 2

Printed in the United States of America

*To those individuals who during the past thirty years
have shared with me their personal struggles with anger
and in so doing
forced me to search for answers
to the troublesome experience of anger*

CONTENTS

FROM ONE SIDE TO ANOTHER

Whether our anger is valid (definitive) or distorted, we must express it positively; we must take loving, beneficial actions as we process our anger. "From One Side to Another" contains summaries and lists that show you how to do that.

ACKNOWLEDGMENTS

*F*ew people want to admit that they have a problem with anger. Most of us readily see the mismanagement of anger on the part of others, but seldom see it in ourselves. I want to acknowledge my debt to hundreds of individuals who in the privacy of my office have shared their tendency toward explosion or implosion of anger. They realized that their negative methods of responding to anger were having destructive effects on those whom they loved, and they sincerely wanted help. Many came with a deep sense of guilt and failure.

As noted in the dedication, their openness forced me to give attention to the whole matter of understanding and processing anger. Their willingness to be vulnerable has made this book possible. Without them, I would not have begun the search that led me to the discovery that anger is the other side of love.

I am also deeply indebted to Tricia Kube, my administrative assistant for fifteen years, who not only computerized the manuscript, but also daily answered numerous phone calls and did other administrative duties that allowed me time to write. Her assistance through the years has been of immeasurable worth to my ministry.

The Moody Press team has done their usual excellent job of encouraging, supporting, and guiding my efforts. Jim Vincent again assisted me greatly in his editorial suggestions. Bill Soderberg produced the discussion questions that will allow the book to be useful in adult study groups. Greg Thornton and Jim Bell were my constant encouragers. My thanks also to William Thrasher, Moody Press general manager, for the title of this book.

Finally, I express my appreciation to Karolyn, my wife for thirty-eight years, who has stood with me through the pain and joys of life. On this project, as with others, she could not have been more supportive. Never complaining about my hours in the office, she always supported my efforts and prayed on my behalf. "Her children arise and call her blessed; her husband . . . praises her" (Proverbs 31:28).

Introduction

UNDERSTANDING AND PROCESSING ANGER

$\mathcal{V}$isit your local library and you will likely find numerous volumes written on the topic of anger. Examine the periodicals index and you will find that every major magazine has had feature articles on anger within the last twelve months. Why then would I venture to write another book on anger?

Two reasons compel me. First, most of what has been written does not deal with two fundamental questions: (1) What is the origin of anger, and (2) what is the purpose of anger? Why do men and women experience the emotion of anger? The two go together. Understanding the origin of anger is essential to understanding the purpose of anger, and understanding the purpose of anger is essential to learning how to process anger in a constructive manner.

The few books and articles that do raise the question of origins tend to see anger as a survival technique in man's early evolutionary development. Anger is "nature's way" of preparing man to respond in times of danger. As one who holds an undergraduate and graduate degree in the field of anthropology, I believe this view is woefully inadequate. In the first place, it ignores the Christian worldview. Second, even if one accepts a naturalistic worldview, it does not adequately explain the psychological aspects of anger.

Among contemporary Christians, there exists great confusion about the emotion of anger. Much of this confusion, in my opinion, flows from a misunderstanding of the origin of anger. Much Christian literature has focused on "how to control anger" without an adequate understanding of the source of anger. I am convinced that our efforts at controlling anger will be much more effective if we have a clearer understanding of the source of anger.

So what is the origin of anger? The answer comes in chapter 1. The origin may surprise you, and it suggests anger's purpose, which is described in chapter 2.

There is a second motivating factor for writing *The Other Side of Love*. It's to help adults, especially married adults, in their family relationships. For almost thirty years now, I have been involved in marriage and family counseling. I have worked with hundreds of families dealing with multiple family problems. In almost all cases, lack of understanding in processing anger has been a key ingredient in family dysfunction. When adults know how to positively process their own anger, they not only create a more secure environment for the family, they also have greater potential for teaching their children how to process anger. Equally important, they are able to have a productive work environment, with healthy relationships and responses to coworkers. Where adults have not learned to process their anger, there is almost always marital and family turmoil, sometimes spilling over to work or other settings.

In the Western world, a common remedy is to seek counseling. Indeed, in America the counseling office has become the major forum for learning to process anger. Unfortunately, most people do not go for counseling until their mismanagement of anger has gotten them into serious trouble. Thousands of others who are already in serious trouble never go for counseling at all. Perhaps you cannot (because of time, money, or fear) step into the counselor's office. I believe that much of what is learned in the counseling office could be learned in the living room if adults had adequate information. This book is an attempt to put into readable form the insights and techniques which have helped hundreds of couples and single adults discover a better way to process anger. The names of all clients have been changed, but their situations and conversations are real. At times, you may recognize issues and responses similar to your own. All of us can learn much about processing our anger more effectively.

I desire that this volume will help readers gain a Christian perspective on anger and from this perspective be able to forge a positive response to their own anger. I also desire that *The Other Side of Love* will provide interested individuals with a tool that will stimulate group discussion and workshops on the topic of anger. Study questions conclude each chapter to help you review key ideas and apply them to your life. I am convinced that much can be learned about anger in an educational setting (your Sunday school class, small group, or seminar) as well as in the counseling office. In fact, this must happen if we are going to turn the tide on the epidemic of verbal and physical abuse that characterizes our generation.

Anger, we will see, is the other side of love. Whereas love draws you toward the other person; anger sets you against the person. Yet anger has positive purposes, and anger can and should be channeled toward good outcomes. The conclusions you will find here derive mainly from my own counseling and the study of Scriptures. (Where appropriate, I will also reference contemporary psychological research.) The Scriptures not only give us didactic teaching about the subject of anger, but they are filled with examples of how people handled anger: both negatively and positively. Most important, the Scriptures reveal the anger of God and how His anger relates to His loving yet holy nature. And in the chapters that follow we will examine how our anger is similar to and different from God's anger.

The Other Side of Love is a biblically based view of anger. It will look at anger's origin and purpose and offer practical help in bringing our anger under the lordship of Christ. When we do that—when we take anger over to the side of love—we accomplish His good purposes.

Chapter 1

WHY DO
PEOPLE
GET ANGRY?

*B*ill was sitting in my office on a hot summer day. He was well dressed, but I noticed his right foot was shoeless. I soon found out why.

"Dr. Chapman, I've got to have help," he began. "I've known for a long time that my anger was getting out of control but Saturday was the last straw. For fifteen minutes, I tried to get my lawn mower started. I checked the gas, I checked the oil, I put in a new spark plug, and still it wouldn't start. Finally, I got so exasperated that I stepped back and kicked the beast. I broke two toes and cut a third. Sitting on the steps in pain, I said to myself, 'That was really stupid.'

"At the time I didn't know I had broken my toes. Later in the doctor's office, I said to myself, 'That was *really* stupid.' So here I am with my toes all bandaged up. I'm embarrassed. I can't tell people what really happened, so I've been saying, 'I had an accident with a lawn mower.' Most people think I cut my toe on the lawn mower blade so they are feeling sorry for me. I don't tell them the truth. I'd rather have them feeling sorry for me than laughing at me. I'm embarrassed to tell you the truth, but I know that I've got to be honest if I'm going to get help.

"This is not the first time I've lost my temper," Bill admitted. "I've said some pretty nasty things to my wife and children in the past. I don't think I have ever physically abused them, but I've come close."

In the course of our conversation I discovered that Bill was highly educated, holding an MBA degree. He was married with two children, profitably employed, and owned a nice house in suburbia. Bill was an active member of his church and well respected in the community. Yet Bill had a habit of "blowing his cool."

Thousands of men can readily identify with Bill. They have "been there and done that." Unfortunately, many of them are not as honest as Bill, and even fewer of them are willing to reach out for help. Of course, this is not a men-only problem. I want you to meet Brooke.

Brooke, an attractive thirty-three-year-old mother of two preschoolers, loved her husband, Glen, an up-and-coming attorney. The couple had been married eight years. Brooke was a certified public accountant but had chosen to put her career on hold until the children started school.

"I think I made a mistake," she told me. "I don't think I am cut out to be a mother. I always wanted children, but now that I've got them, I don't like the way I treat them. And I don't like what they do to me. I don't ever remember being angry or losing my temper before I had children. I always considered myself to be 'in control' of my emotions. But I have to admit, I have often 'lost it' with my children. I hate myself when I do that, and I know that it's not good for the children."

"What do you do when you lose it with the children?" I inquired.

"Different things," she said. "Sometimes, I yell at them. Sometimes, I spank them really hard. The other day I picked up Ginger and shook her. That really scared me. I had just seen on television the day before the report of a mother who actually killed her child by shaking her. I don't want to hurt my children. I love them, but I just lose control. I wish Glen would keep the kids and give me a break, but he is so stressed in his job that he says he doesn't feel like keeping the kids. I think maybe I should go back to work and let someone else take care of the children."

As I talked further with Brooke, I discovered that she was angry not only with her children's behavior but also with Glen for giving her so little help. She was angry at herself for choosing to be a full-time mom, and ultimately she was angry with God for allowing her to be a mother. "He should have known that I would not be able to handle this," she said.

By now Brooke was crying. To be honest, I too felt like crying, as I remembered the hundreds of mothers who have passed through my office over the last thirty years looking for a place to resign.

Bill with his broken toes and Brooke with her broken heart live in very different worlds; however, what they hold in common is the human experience of intense anger and their seeming inability to handle it. Both knew that their anger had led them to inappropriate behavior, but neither knew what to do about it. Thus, they suffered physically and emotionally from their destructive responses to anger. In addition, family members who lived with them also suffered the fallout of their negative behavior.

ANGER: A UNIVERSAL EXPERIENCE

In later chapters I want to explain what Bill and Brooke learned about how to respond to anger in a more productive manner, but first, we must go back to the beginning. We must answer the questions, "What is anger, and what is its origin?" Anthropologists have discovered that anger is pan-human; that is, anger is experienced in all cultures throughout the world. Thus when I speak of the origin of anger, I am not talking about reasons why a particular person was angry on a particular day. I am seeking rather to address the question, "Why is anger a universal experience among all people? What is the origin of man's capacity for anger?"

Within a given culture, anger is not limited to a particular group of people. People of all ages and social status experience anger. Meredith, a single adult, is angry with her mother, who seeks to manipulate her behavior. Brian, a high school student, is angry at his teacher who gave him a D on his report card. Tina, a fifteen-year-old, is angry; she feels that her parents treat her like a ten-year-old kid. Barbara, an eighty-five-year-old grandmother, is angry with her oldest son, who seldom comes to see her; she's also angry with her daughter, who comes every day but never stays long enough. Marvin, a pastor, is angry with church leadership who respond negatively to his best ideas. Bethany is only three years old, but she is angry with her mother, who took away her favorite toy.

From whence all this anger?

WHAT IS ANGER?

First, let's seek to clarify what we mean by anger. *Merriam-Webster's New Collegiate Dictionary* (sixth edition) describes anger as "a strong passion or emotion of displeasure, and usually antagonism, excited by a sense of injury or insult." Although we normally think of anger as an emotion, it is in reality more than an emotion. Anger involves the emotions, the body, the mind, and the will, all of which are stimulated by some event in the individual's life.

Anger is always stimulated by an event. We don't sit down and say, "I think I will now experience anger." Anger is a response to some event in life that causes us irritation, frustration, pain, or other displeasure. He comes home late; she fails to record a check; he fails to take out the garbage. You agree to meet at 6:30 P.M. It is now 7:30 P.M. and he/she has not arrived. Thousands of events have the potential for stimulating anger. Once the event has happened, the emotions respond.

Typically anger is a cluster of emotions involving such feelings as disappointment, hurt, rejection, embarrassment, and other similar feelings. All of these clustered feelings we call anger. Anger is the emotion that typically pits you against the person, place, or thing that stimulated the emotion. It is the opposite of the feeling of love. Love draws you toward the person; anger sets you against the person.

But the mind is also active from the very beginning. For example, when he comes home late and does not call, she reasons, *If he cared he'd call. He knows how hard I work to have dinner ready on time. He has no concern for me. All he thinks about is his work. Obviously I don't mean much to him. Why did I ever marry such a selfish man?* A husband reasons, *I mow the grass, wash the car, and take care of the baby while she goes shopping with her mother and I don't even get a thanks!* He is angry.

Meanwhile, Mary sits quietly in her supervisor's office as he proceeds to inform her that her work has not been satisfactory and that if she cannot increase her productivity, he will be forced to terminate her employment. Her mind engages, even though at first she says nothing. *It's because I'm a single woman,* she reasons. *I know I work harder than the men, but he picks on me. He hasn't liked me from the start. It's not fair.* With these thoughts, Mary is also experiencing strong, negative emotions.

The body also gets in on the experience of anger. The body's autonomic nervous system "gets the adrenaline flowing." Depending upon the level of anger, any or all of the following may happen physically. The adrenal glands release two hormones: epinephrine (adrenaline) and norepinephrine (noradrenaline). These two chemicals seem to give people the arousal, the tenseness, the excitement, the heat of anger. "These hormones in turn stimulate changes in heart rate, blood pressure, lung function, and digestive tract activity which further add to the general arousal feelings people have when they are angry."[1] It is these physiological changes that give people the feeling of being overwhelmed by anger and being unable to control it.

Note that the emotions, thoughts, and physiological changes are all intertwined. Together they compose what we call anger. Typically this anger is then expressed in behavior: words or actions. So Bill kicks the lawn mower; Brooke shakes her preschooler; the mother berates the teenager who arrives home late; the wife withdraws in silence from the husband who angered her, etc. Let me mention here what we will develop more fully in later chapters. Although we have little control over our emotional and physiological responses to a troubling event, we can learn to control our thoughts—the way we interpret these events—and our behavior—our words and actions.

Later we will see how we can control and channel our thoughts and behavior. Our purpose at the moment is to clarify the components of anger. In summary, anger is the emotions, thoughts, and physical tenseness we experience when we believe that something or someone is treating us or someone else unfairly.

WHAT IS THE ORIGIN OF ANGER?

Let us now turn our attention to the question, What is the origin of anger? Or, to put it another way, Why do we experience anger? Anger is a pervasive human experience, and to know its source is the beginning of knowing how to deal with it.

I believe that the human capacity for anger is rooted in the nature of God. Please do not think that I am being disrespectful of God. On the contrary, I stand in deep reverence of God when I suggest that human anger is rooted in the divine nature. Further, I am not suggesting that anger is an essential part of the nature of God. I am suggesting that anger derives from two aspects of God's divine nature: God's holiness and God's love.

The Scriptures proclaim that God is holy. (See, for example, 1 Peter 1:16; Leviticus 11:44–45.) The word *holy* means *set apart from sin.* Whether we are talking about God the Father, God the Son, or God the Spirit, there is no sin in the nature of God. The New Testament writer said of Jesus that He was "tempted in every way, just as we are—yet was without sin" (Hebrews 4:15).

A second fundamental characteristic of the nature of God is love. John the apostle summarized the whole teaching of Scripture when he said simply, "God *is* love" (1 John 4:8, italics added). Please note that love is an adjective and not a noun. Love is not to be equated with God; rather in His essential nature God is loving. This is not simply the New Testament concept of God. From beginning to end, the Scriptures reveal God as committed to the well-being of His creatures. It is God's nature to love.

It is from these two divine characteristics that God's anger is derived. Please note: The Scriptures never say, "God is anger." That statement is not in fact true. Anger is not a part of the essential nature of God. However, the Scriptures often indicate that God experiences anger. The word *anger* is found 455 times in the Old Testament; 375 of these times it is used of God's anger. In fact, the psalmist said, "God is angry with the wicked every day" (Psalm 7:11 KJV).

Nor was God's anger limited to Old Testament times. Read the life of Jesus and you will see numerous occasions where Jesus experienced anger. (For example, see Mark 3:1–5; John 2:13–17.) Because God is holy and because God is love, God necessarily experiences anger. His love seeks only the good of His creatures. His holiness stands forever against sin. All of God's moral laws are based upon His holiness and His love; that is, they are always aligned with what is right, and they are always for the good of His creatures. God desires man to do what is right and enjoy the benefits. He said to ancient Israel, "See, I set before you today life and prosperity, death and destruction. For I command you today to love the Lord your God, to walk in his ways, and to keep his commands, decrees and laws; then you will live and increase, and the Lord your God will bless you in the land you are entering to possess" (Deuteronomy 30:15–16).

Knowing the detrimental effects of man's sin, God's anger is stirred. It is God's concern for justice and righteousness (both of which grow out of His holiness and His love) that stimulate God's anger. Thus when God sees evil, God experiences anger. Anger is His logical response to injustice or unrighteousness.

So what does all of this have to do with human anger? The Scriptures say that we are made "in the image of God" (Genesis 1:27). Though that image was marred by man's Fall, it was not erased. People still bear the imprint of God's image deep within their souls. Thus, even though we are fallen, we still have some concern for justice and rightness. That is, people are moral creatures. In spite of modern man's attempt to reduce humans to an amoral creature, such a view is not consistent with reality. No matter how far a person may fall, he still has some concern for rightness. Find the most pagan man you know and follow him for a week, and you will hear him make such statements as: "That's not right. He shouldn't do that to her. She treated him wrongly." Steal his car and see if he expresses anger. Murder his daughter or wife or girlfriend and you will find that suddenly he is an extremely moral creature, condemning your action outright.

Listen to the young child who is beginning to put words into sentences and you will soon hear the child say, "That's not fair, Mommy." Where did the child obtain that moral judgment? I suggest that it is stamped deep within his nature, tempered by parental teaching to be sure, but the child knows when he/she has been wronged and will express it freely.

Anger, then, is the emotion that arises whenever we encounter what we perceive to be wrong. The emotional, physiological, and cognitive dimensions of anger leap to the front burner of our experience when we encounter injustice.

Why does a wife experience anger toward her husband? Because in her mind he has disappointed, embarrassed, humiliated, or rejected her. In short, "he has done her wrong." Why do teenagers experience anger toward parents? Because the teenager perceives that the parents have been unfair, unloving, unkind—that the parents have done wrong. Why do men get angry with lawn mowers? Because the lawn mower is not "working right." The machine, or its manufacturer, has done him wrong. Why do men blow horns when the traffic light turns green? Because they reason that the person in front of them "should be paying attention to the light and should have accelerated two seconds earlier." In short, they are not doing "right."

Try to remember the last time you experienced anger and ask the question, "Why did I get angry?" Chances are your answer will mention some injustice. Someone or something did not treat you fairly. Something was wrong. Your anger may have been directed toward a person, an object, a situation, yourself, or God, but in every instance someone or something treated you wrongly. We are not here discussing whether your perception of wrong is valid or invalid. We will deal with that in a later chapter. What we are establishing here is that anger originates in the perception that something is wrong and that this sense of morality (some things are right and some things are wrong) finds its root in the fact that we are created in the image of a God who is holy and has established moral law for the good of His creatures.

Anger is not evil; anger is not sinful; anger is not a part of our fallen nature; anger is not Satan at work in our lives. Quite the contrary. Anger is evidence that we are made in God's image; it demonstrates that we still have some concern for justice and righteousness in spite of our fallen estate. The capacity for anger is strong evidence that we are more than mere animals. It reveals our concern for rightness, justice, and fairness. The experience of anger is evidence of our nobility, not our depravity.

We should thank God for our capacity to experience anger. When one ceases to experience anger, one has lost his sense of moral concern. Without moral concern, the world would be a dreadful place indeed. That brings us to our second major concern, namely, what is the purpose of anger?

NOTE

1. Mark T. Crosgrove, *Counseling for Anger* (Dallas: Word, 1988), 30.

FOR DISCUSSION

1. We have—and will—experience anger throughout our lives. Try to recall instances where you became angry as a young child, as a teenager, and as an adult. Share one of these instances with your group. After several have spoken, look at examples from the three age groupings and compare the responses to anger in each of the three. Is age and maturity an indicator of an improved response to handling anger? What elements of response seem to be common to all three situations?

2. Although anger is largely thought of as an emotion, it affects us physically, mentally, and psychologically as well. List some physical effects you have observed in others who become angry. Discuss the physical effects of anger and how they influence the way we process anger.

3. God often experiences anger, but anger is not an essential element of His nature. Rather, His anger derives from God's holiness and love. Still, such anger may seem contrary to His loving nature. Read the account of the Israelites besieging Ai (Joshua 7). Does God's anger at the people seem reasonable? Is His anger processed in accordance with His love and holiness? Discuss within the group.

4. *Processing your anger:* You live in an apartment building. The apartment has an unwritten rule that asks residents not to use the washer and dryer after 10:00 P.M. This is to avoid disturbing residents in the nearby apartments. Although you started doing laundry well before 10:00, you will not be complete until 10:30. When you go into the laundry room at 10:15, you discover the dryer has been turned off and your wet clothes are in a heap on the floor. Discuss among the group how you might resolve your anger. List responses and collectively select the response you think will best help you process your anger. Save your notes for comparison in successive chapters.

Chapter 2

WHAT IS
THE PURPOSE
OF ANGER?

$\mathcal{A}$nger is a universal human experience, and God Himself often experiences anger. Those two facts, affirmed in chapter 1, lead us to conclude that there must be a foundational purpose for human anger. Since the capacity for human anger is a reflection of the image of the creator, we are compelled to ask the question "What is God's purpose for human anger?"

I believe the answer is clear: *Human anger is designed of God to motivate us to take constructive action* in the face of wrongdoing or when facing injustice. The reason this has not always been abundantly clear to Christians is that in our fallen estate, our perception of injustice is not always valid. That is, not all human anger is toward actual wrongdoing. The fact that our fallen nature is egocentric (centered on oneself) rather than theocentric (centered on God) often leads us to experience anger at anything that does not go our way. We will talk about valid and invalid anger in another chapter, but our purpose here is to return to the foundational question, "What is God's purpose in human anger?" The answer is: Anger is designed to motivate us to take positive, loving action when we encounter injustice. This, I believe, is illustrated by God Himself.

GOD'S RESPONSE TO ANGER

When we examine the record of God's anger in both the Old and New Testaments, we find that His patterned response always involves loving action. In the Old Testament, He typically sent a prophet to proclaim to the people His displeasure with their evil deeds and to call them to repentance. If the people repented, God's anger subsided and all was well. If, however, they did not repent, God took additional action. God's message to Jeremiah demonstrates this. "Go, proclaim this message toward the north: 'Return, faithless Israel,' declares the Lord, 'I will frown on you no longer, for I am merciful,' declares the Lord. 'I will not be angry forever. Only acknowledge your guilt . . . . Return, faithless people,' declares the Lord, 'for I am your husband'" (Jeremiah 3:12–14). Israel had forsaken truth and followed lies. God's anger motivated Him to send Jeremiah to call the people to repentance.

God took similar action in sending Jonah to Nineveh. The people of Nineveh knew God's reputation. When Jonah proclaimed the message of destruction in forty days, the Scriptures say, "The Ninevites believed God. They declared a fast, and all of them, from the greatest to the least, put on sackcloth." Soon the king declared, "Let everyone call urgently on God. Let them give up their evil ways and their violence. Who knows? God may yet relent and with compassion turn from his fierce anger so that we will not perish." The people of Nineveh knew that God's anger was always driven by His love. So the Scriptures record, "When God saw what they did and how they turned from their evil ways, he had compassion and did not bring upon them the destruction he had threatened" (Jonah 3:5, 8–10).

God's anger was expressed in positive action—declaring to the evildoer that all evil would be punished. Because of God's love for them, He could not allow injustice to go unpunished. However, when the people of Nineveh repented and turned from their evil ways, God's compassion forgave them. The wrong had been righted; God's anger had served its positive purpose. Throughout the Old Testament, this pattern of positive, loving action can be seen as God's response to anger. When people responded in repentance to the condemning message of God through the prophets, God always freely forgave. But when people did not respond and continued in their evil ways, God took further action—sometimes using swarms of locusts to eat the crops before harvest; sometimes famine and fire; sometimes foreign powers who would capture and take His people into slavery. But always the message was clear: God is doing this because of your sin. (See, for example, Amos 1–2.)

Some contemporary students of the Bible have questioned God's severe acts of judgment on His people Israel and their neighbors. They have read into these acts the picture of a severe God who has no love but only justice. However, upon closer examination, one discovers that when God used such severe measures it was for the ultimate good of His creatures. His holiness will not allow God to remain silent when men are involved in evil activity, and His love always seeks to express His anger for the larger good of mankind. When evil became so entrenched in a given culture and the people's hearts hardened to the call of God, God's judgment was severe in order to demonstrate to all the neighboring nations that such evil would not be tolerated forever. In destroying the cesspools of man's severe evil, God sought to prevent other nations from following the same destructive road. All His actions were just and all His actions were loving.

JESUS' RESPONSE TO ANGER

When we turn to the New Testament and examine the life of Jesus, we find that He too followed the same pattern in responding to His own anger. He took positive, loving action against the evil that had stimulated His anger. Perhaps the best known of these events was Jesus' experience in the temple in Jerusalem when He saw the merchants buying and selling oxen, sheep, and doves. He said, "It is written, . . . 'My house will be called a house of prayer,' but you are making it a 'den of robbers'" (Matthew 21:13). Clearly it was their wrong behavior that stimulated His anger. Much earlier in His ministry, Jesus had upbraided the money changers: "How dare you turn my Father's house into a market!" (John 2:16). John the apostle recorded that Jesus made a whip of cords, drove them from the temple area, and "scattered the coins of the money changers and overturned their tables" (verse 15).

Some would ask, "Where was Jesus' spirit of forgiveness?" We can without question assume that had they repented, He would have forgiven. But remember God's forgiveness is always in response to man's repentance. His action demonstrated not only to the merchants but also to the religious leaders that what was going on was inappropriate for the temple of God. In fact, John records, "His disciples remembered that it is written: 'Zeal for your house will consume me'" (2:17; see Psalm 69:9). The disciples clearly saw Jesus' anger being expressed, and they attributed it to His righteous and deep concern that His Father's house be a place of prayer rather than a place of merchandise.

On another occasion Jesus was in the synagogue on the Sabbath, and a man came to Him with a paralyzed hand. The Pharisees were looking for an occasion to accuse Jesus of breaking the Sabbath law, so Jesus asked the question, "Which is lawful on the Sabbath: to do good or to do evil, to save life or to kill?" The Pharisees remained silent and Mark records that Jesus "looked around at them in anger and, deeply distressed at their stubborn hearts, said to the man, 'Stretch out your hand.' He stretched it out, and his hand was completely restored" (Mark 3:4–5). Jesus' anger was stimulated by the Pharisees' legalistic thinking, which placed the keeping of Sabbath laws above ministry to human need. His action was to heal the man in front of their faces, rejecting their evil thinking and graphically demonstrating in front of everyone that human ministry is more important than religious observances. Thus, the divine model is clear: God's response to anger is always to take loving action, to seek to stop the evil, and to redeem the evildoer.

OUR RESPONSE TO ANGER: TO SEEK RIGHTEOUSNESS AND REFORM

Now let's return to the human scene. I am not in any way suggesting that we are little gods. What I am suggesting is that we are creatures made in God's image and, because of that, we have at least on some level a concern for righteousness, fairness, and justice. Whenever we encounter that which we believe to be unrighteous, unkind, or unjust, we experience anger. I believe that in God's design *this anger is to motivate us to take positive, loving action to seek to set the wrong right;* and where there has been a relationship, to restore the relationship with the wrongdoer. Anger is not designed to stimulate us to do destructive things to the people who may have wronged us nor does it give us license to say or do destructive things to our neighbors. Anger's fundamental purpose is to motivate us to positive, loving action that will leave things better than we found them.

First, let us examine this in the whole area of social reform. Anger has been the great motivator for all social reform. Most readers will be familiar with the organization MADD (Mothers Against Drunk Drivers). Do you have any idea why this organization was established? I suggest to you that it was born out of anger. Mothers watched their sons and daughters being killed in the streets by drunken drivers. When these drivers came to trial, they were given a slap on the wrist, given perhaps a small fine, and returned to the streets the next day.

The mothers said, "This is not right." The founder, Candy Lightner, was shocked when a drunken driver plowed his vehicle into her thirteen-year-old daughter, leaving little Cari dead. Later her shock and grief turned into intense anger, when a California judge gave the repeat-offender drunk driver a light sentence. She and other outraged mothers soon formed MADD. It was this anger, stimulated by the injustice that they observed, which motivated Mrs. Lightner and other outraged mothers to establish a national organization which later grew to more than four hundred chapters.

Initially, their approach was to take turns sitting in the courtroom when those who were charged with "driving under the influence" were being tried. They looked in the eyes of the judge, the lawyers, and the drunken drivers. Their presence stimulated judges to think twice before returning the license of a drunken driver. They also pressured state legislators to enact tougher laws against drunk driving. I don't think I have to tell you that the penalty of driving under the influence has been more stringent the last few years and more driver's licenses have been removed from those driving under the influence than ever before. All because some mothers got angry. MADD continues to seek judicial and legislative reforms.

The organization SADD (Students Against Driving Drunk) formed in a similar manner. Students were upset about the harm caused by drunken student drivers; they began to say, "It is not right to allow a fellow student to drive while under the influence of alcohol." These students began to organize and committed themselves to have a designated, sober driver who would volunteer to drive the intoxicated student home. They took positive, loving action in response to their anger.

The abolition of slavery in England and America came about because a significant number of people felt anger about social conditions. In England, the Society of Friends (Quakers) started an antislavery movement in 1671; American Quakers took up the fight in 1696. Thomas Clarkson and William Wilberforce persuaded the British government to pass a bill against the slave trade in 1807. Slavery was abolished in all British colonies in 1833. In March 1807, the United States prohibited further importation of slaves after January 1, 1808. This act legally ended the overseas trade in slaves, but slavery itself continued until the end of the Civil War. In the United States, Lincoln's Emancipation Proclamation declared all slaves free in 1863.

The inhumane practice of slavery would not have ended without anger. A significant number of people said within their own hearts, "This is not right."

They experienced the emotion of anger and moved out to take positive, loving steps to free those who were in bondage.

This is in keeping with God's desires as stated through the prophet Isaiah, "I have chosen: to loose the chains of injustice and untie the cords of the yoke, to set the oppressed free and break every yoke . . . to share your food with the hungry and to provide the poor wanderer with shelter—when you see the naked, to clothe him, and not to turn away from your own flesh and blood" (Isaiah 58:6–7). Anger's purpose is to motivate us to respond to the injustices of life with constructive, loving action and do all that is in our power to see that justice prevails. Our actions, however, must always be guided by love.

Anger has also been at the root of religious reform movements. During the Protestant Reformation, anger motivated Luther and others to rebel against the established church. In their minds, the practices of the Christian church of their day were not in keeping with Scripture and thus were wrong. Their anger was strong enough to take some of them to a martyr's death in opposition to what they believed to be wrong. I submit that all great social and religious reforms have been born out of anger.

MOTIVATED BY INJUSTICE, GUIDED BY LOVE

On the personal level, the pattern is no different, though the approach will vary with each situation. Let's return to Brooke, whom we met in the last chapter. She is angry with her preschool children because of what she considers to be their inappropriate behavior, mad at her husband because he doesn't give her adequate help at home, mad at herself because she made the choice to be at home with her children, and ultimately mad at God because in her mind He allowed her to get into this mess. At the moment, we are not concerned with what specific actions Brooke should take; we are simply asking the question, "What is the purpose of Brooke's anger?" I suggest that it is to motivate her to take positive, loving action to deal with what she considers to be unkind, inequitable, unfair, and inhumane. She is not to ignore her anger. Anger is like a red light flashing on the dash of a car. It indicates that something needs attention. What she does to the flashing light of anger is extremely important and will be discussed in the next chapter.

Thus anger itself is good. It's a powerful and positive motivator, useful to move us toward loving action to right wrongs and correct injustice. But it can become a raging, uncontrolled force. When it is channeled correctly, however, it moves us to the other side—to the side of love. We can and must make our anger productive in our lives.

The danger is that it can become counterproductive, working against us. Remember Bill and his anger with his lawn mower? His action, a swift kick to the mower's side, yielded him physical pain and embarrassment.

He had spent fifteen minutes pulling, priming, and pampering the lawn mower, but still it refused to start. Bill experienced anger. Why? Because the lawn mower was not performing the way it was designed to perform. "It's not working." Lawn mower engines are supposed to run so that grass can be cut. Bill couldn't reach his legitimate objective because the lawn mower refused to cooperate. When a man only has two hours to get the job done, "It's just not right for a lawn mower to rebel." At the moment, let's waive the issue as to whether Bill's anger is valid (and whether there are other reasons that may have also fed into Bill's anger). What is a man to do when angry with a lawn mower?

Obviously, Bill's action was not positive and not loving. He was not looking out for his own best interest when he planted his toes against the hard metal of the lawn mower. It didn't hurt the lawn mower since it was an inanimate object, but Bill will be suffering the results of his inappropriate response to anger for several weeks.

Later we will look more fully at what Bill might have done, but at present our question is, "What is the purpose of Bill's anger?" If we apply the model developed in this chapter, we will be compelled to say that Bill's anger is to motivate him to take constructive action to get the lawn mower to run. This may have involved walking to a neighbor who knew more about engines than Bill, or calling a repair shop, or borrowing a neighbor's lawn mower to get the job done today while placing his mower in the shop.

Of course, the difficulty is that all of these wonderfully positive purposes of anger seem to elude us in the heat of anger. We forget about "setting things right" and end up "making things worse." This brings us to the next pressing question: "How can we process anger in a positive way?"

FOR DISCUSSION

1. The example of Jonah delivering God's call for repentance to the people of Nineveh demonstrates that God's anger is driven by His love. He desires love, but requires obedience from His children so that they can be in fellowship with Him. How does God respond to you when you are not in step with His will? Is the lesson you learn easy or hard? Share with your group a specific example from your past where your actions were at cross-purposes with the Lord. Point to where you can see His love at work in specific, tangible ways.

2. God's anger appears harsh many times in the Bible. Compare God's reaction to the Israelite's commissioning of the golden calf (Exodus 32) and Saul's conversion (Acts 9), and discuss how His reactions differed. Did His differing response indicate differing standards for His demand for loving obedience? Discuss these ideas within the group and record the similarities and differences in each story. Is God's "bottom line" intent the same for each of these situations?

3. God's anger stems from His love for us and desire that we follow the universal laws He has created for our well-being. In like fashion, we should be similarly motivated when we encounter hatred or injustice. Identify a recent episode where you became angry, yet responded with a compassionate but firm need for correction. It might be an episode in disciplining children, disagreeing with a coworker, or debating a political issue. Identify the steps you took to recognize the problem, the source of anger, and the means used to resolve the issue. Was the anger resolved or is it still present? Share your experience with the group.

4. *Processing your anger:* You are a Christian parent of a child in a public elementary school, attending the monthly Parent Teacher Organization meeting. During the planning for the annual Easter music program, a small group of parents protest having "a religious observance at a public school." The group claims that their children will be forcibly proselytized by the experience. Despite years of recognizing Easter as a Christian holiday in the school program, the administration, leery of litigation, is leaning toward the adoption of a "Rites of Spring Festival" in lieu of the Easter musical. Are you angry? At whom? How would you respond to this situation? Discuss your response within the group.

Chapter 3

HOW CAN I MAKE ANGER PRODUCTIVE?

The following people all feel anger for different reasons. Yet the object of their anger is the same. Can you recognize what it is?

- Brent has worked at the same company for fourteen years. He has worked hard and, in his mind, has given the company more than a fair share. Last week he discovered he had just been passed over a second time for a promotion he had anticipated. He thinks his supervisor is being unfair. He is extremely angry.

- Robert has promised to meet Tricia at the mall to shop for luggage for their upcoming trip. At 6:30, the appointed time, Robert is not in the appointed place. Tricia waits twenty minutes and then decides to look at luggage on her own. She halfheartedly looks at luggage, but she wholeheartedly is angry with Robert, who never shows.

- Sheila is angry with her sixteen-year-old son, Josh, not only because his room looks like a disaster and his grandmother is due in three hours, but also because he's left without telling Sheila where he is going. She has no idea whether he will be back before his grandmother's arrival, and she certainly doesn't have time to clean the room herself. Her anger is getting hotter every time she thinks about his irresponsibility.

- Randy feels extremely angry with Carol because, to use his words, "She never has any time for me. She has time to have lunch with her friends. She's seen more movies with them than with me. I'm tired of coming home to an empty house every night. I wish someone would tell her that she's married."

- Alan's neighbor for the past eight years decided last week to begin re-landscaping his front lawn. In the process of removing shrubs, he removed two that were on Alan's lot. When Alan saw the holes and his shrubbery gone, he was first of all shocked and then he was angry. *Does he think that's his lot?* he reasoned. *Why would he take my shrubs down? Let him do what he wishes with his own yard but he has no right to destroy my shrubs.* His wife, Ellen, gets an earful when she arrives home from work.

- Will and Angie have tickets for the basketball game on Saturday. They have wanted to attend a game all season, but this is the first time their schedules have allowed it. On Thursday night, Angie's mother called asking if they would keep an eye on Angie's ten-year-old brother Saturday afternoon while her parents go to a business outing. Angie told her mother that they were going to the basketball game and she wasn't sure they could get another ticket. Her mother said, "Oh, you can always get tickets. We'll pay for it. Don't worry about it." Before Angie realized what she had done, she had agreed. When she told Will what she had done, he became furious. "There are no additional tickets," he said. "I checked that out today because a friend at the office wanted one. Now we're going to have to miss the game because your stupid mother is not willing to take care of her own child." Will is angry at his mother-in-law for asking and his wife for agreeing.

- Christina is sitting in my office after fourteen years of marriage to Brad. "I don't understand it," she said. "We've been married for fourteen years and we've had a good marriage. Now he tells me he doesn't love me anymore and that he's in love with someone else. How could he be in love with someone else? Just last week he made love to me. How could he do that if he's in love with someone else?" No question about it, Christina is extremely angry.

All these people feel angry toward the same object: someone else. This is the kind of anger we are discussing in this chapter: anger toward someone with whom you have a relationship. It may be a family member, roommate, friend, work associate, neighbor, or anyone with whom you have an ongoing relationship. We will not discuss anger that you experience because of something you hear or see on television, anger that you feel toward another driver when you are in your car, or anger that you feel toward inanimate objects—flat tires, bicycle chains, wrenches, or computers. Nor will we discuss anger that you feel toward animals—squirrels that steal your tomatoes, rabbits that eat your lettuce, raccoons that ravage your garbage can, or deer that, while you are on vacation, eat your entire garden. All of these we will discuss later.

TWO PARAMOUNT QUESTIONS

In processing anger towards someone with whom you have a relationship, two questions are paramount: 1. Is the action I am considering positive; i.e., does it have the potential for dealing with the wrong and healing the relationship? 2. Is the action I'm considering loving; i.e., is it designed for the benefit of the person at whom I am angry?

Since these are the dual purposes of anger, you should always run your contemplated action through this grid: Is it positive and is it loving?

Valid anger, that is, anger which has been stimulated by genuine wrongdoing on the part of the other person, needs to be processed in a positive manner. Later we will discuss the pitfalls of responding to anger with destructive behavior. But in this chapter, I would like to give a plan for processing anger in a constructive manner.

A MODEL FOR MAKING
YOUR ANGER PRODUCTIVE

Dealing with valid anger is a five-step process: (1) consciously acknowledge to yourself that you are angry; (2) restrain your immediate response; (3) locate the focus of your anger; (4) analyze your options; and (5) take constructive action. As we complete each step, we move toward making our anger productive.

FIVE STEPS TO HANDLE VALID ANGER

1. Consciously acknowledge to yourself that you are angry.
2. Restrain your immediate response.
3. Locate the focus of your anger.
4. Analyze your options.
5. Take constructive action.

First, consciously acknowledge to yourself that you are angry. "That's obvious," you might reply. "Anyone would know that I am angry." Perhaps, but the question is, "Are you conscious of your anger?" Because the emotion of anger comes on so suddenly, often we are caught up in a verbal or physical response to the anger before ever consciously acknowledging what is going on inside of us. We are far more likely to make a positive response to our anger if we first acknowledge to ourselves that we are angry.

I suggest that you say the words out loud. "I am angry about this! Now what am I going to do?" Such a statement places the issues squarely on the table. You are now not only aware of your own anger, but you have distinguished for yourself the difference between your anger and the action you are going to take. You have set the stage for applying reason to your anger rather than simply being controlled by your emotions. This is an important first step in processing anger positively.

As simple as this may sound, some Christians have difficulty with this. All their lifetime they have been taught that anger is sin. Thus, to admit that they are angry is to admit that they are sinning. But this is not the biblical perspective on anger. I hope that the first two chapters have made it clear that the experience of anger is not sinful. It is a part of our humanity and reflects the anger experienced by God Himself. Paul stated it clearly when he said, "In your anger do not sin" (Ephesians 4:26). The challenge is not "Don't get angry," but the challenge is not to sin when we are angry.

That is precisely the topic we are addressing in this chapter. "How do I keep from sinning when I am angry?" Or to put it in a positive way, "How do I respond to my anger so that my actions will be constructive?" I believe that consciously and verbally acknowledging to yourself that you are angry is a first step in reaching this objective.

FIVE STEPS TO HANDLE VALID ANGER

1. Consciously acknowledge to yourself that you are angry.
2. Restrain your immediate response.
3. Locate the focus of your anger.
4. Analyze your options.
5. Take constructive action.

Second, restrain your immediate response. If when we are angry we simply "go with the flow," we will likely have a negative and destructive response to anger. Very few adults have learned how to control and direct their anger. Most of us follow the patterns we learned in childhood by observing our parents or other significant adults. These patterns tend to cluster around two extremes: verbal or physical venting on the one hand or withdrawal and silence on the other. Both are destructive. We will look at these and other patterns in a later chapter.

For most of us, anger-control will be something we must learn as adults, and that means unlearning old patterns. Thus, restraining our immediate response is extremely important in establishing new patterns. Restraining our response is not the same as storing our anger. It is refusing to take the action that we typically take when feeling angry. Solomon wisely wrote, "A fool gives full vent to his anger, but a wise man keeps himself under control" (Proverbs 29:11). And again, "People with good sense restrain their anger" (Proverbs 19:11 NLT). Or consider the soberness of this proverb by Solomon: "A quick-tempered man does foolish things" (14:17). Someone has said, "Speak when you are angry and you will make the best speech you will ever regret." Most of us have had the experience of saying or doing things in the immediate flush of anger that we later regretted but unfortunately were unable to erase. Far better to learn to restrain our immediate response.

From time to time I meet people in my marriage seminars who say to me, "Dr. Chapman, I cannot control my anger. When I get angry, I am overwhelmed. I cannot restrain my response. I simply go berserk." While I am sympathetic with what the person is saying and I understand the overpowering nature of anger once it starts to roll, I believe that this is an ill-founded statement. It is true that once we begin to release anger in a destructive way verbally or physically, it's difficult to stop the flow of lava. But there is that moment before the red-hot words begin to flow that we can train ourselves to restrain that response.

Did your mother give you this commonsense advice? "When you are angry, count to ten before you do or say anything." It is good advice, but many of us may need to count to 100 or even 1,000. This long delay may quell the fire within. Many have found this to be a workable technique in helping them restrain their response.

I suggest that you count out loud. If you are in the presence of the person at whom you are angry, I suggest you leave. Take a walk as you count. About halfway around the block when you come to 597, you will probably be in a mental and emotional state where you can stop and say, "I am angry about this. Now what am I going to do?" For the Christian, this is the time to pray, "Lord, you know that I am angry. I believe that what they have done is wrong. Please help me make a wise decision about how to respond in this situation." Then with God you begin to look at your options.

Another technique that I have often shared at my marriage seminars is to call "time-out" when you realize that you are angry. This may be expressed verbally by simply saying the words "time-out," or it may be expressed visually by the time-out sign often seen in athletic events on television in which outstretched fingers on both hands are brought together to form a *T*. It is your symbol for saying, "I'm feeling angry right now and I don't want to lose it, so 'time-out.'" If both of you understand that this is a positive technique not a cop-out on the situation, then you can accept this as a positive step in controlling anger. Please note that the time-out is not for three months; it is simply for a brief time to give you an opportunity to get in control of your emotions so that you can approach the situation with constructive action.

FIVE STEPS TO HANDLE VALID ANGER

1. Consciously acknowledge to yourself that you are angry.
2. Restrain your immediate response.
3. Locate the focus of your anger.
4. Analyze your options.
5. Take constructive action.

Step three takes place as you are restraining your immediate response. While you are on your "time-out" and after you have counted to 100—or

1,000—*locate the focus of your anger.* If you are angry with your spouse, ask yourself the following questions: Why am I so angry? Is it what my spouse has said or done? Is it the way he or she is talking? Is it the way he or she is looking at me? Does my spouse's behavior remind me of my mother or father? Is my anger toward my spouse influenced by something that happened at work today or in my childhood years ago?

Sheila realized that her anger toward her son Josh (who had failed to clean his room before leaving) was tied to her mother's arrival in three hours. Her mind rushed back to a scene years ago in which her mother glared at her and said, "You will never amount to anything. Look, you can't even keep your room cleaned up." That same mother would soon walk through the door and observe Josh's room. Would this be the final evidence that indeed Sheila was a failure? She admitted that if her mother were not coming, Josh's room would not be a big deal to her. In fact, his room was often cluttered. This understanding helped Sheila take a more positive approach to her anger.

The bottom line in locating the focus of your anger is to discover the wrong committed by the person at whom you are angry. What is the person's sin? How has she wronged you? Randy, who said about his wife, Carol, "She never has any time for me. . . . I wish someone would tell her that she's married," is intensely angry, but his anger is not yet focused. When he analyzed his anger, he realized that the issue was not whether Carol should have lunch or go to movies with her friends. His anger really focused on his unmet need for love. In his mind, that was the real issue. A wife should express love to her husband. He did not feel loved. He felt neglected. His anger really focused on Carol's failure to meet his emotional need for love. This insight led him to process his anger in a much more constructive manner.

The secondary issue is, how serious is the offense? Robert's failure to show up at 6:30 P.M. to shop for luggage is certainly not on the same level as Robert having an affair. Some wrongs are minor and some are major. Each calls for a different response. To have the same response to minor issues as one does for major issues is to mismanage one's anger.

You may find it helpful to rate the seriousness of the issue on a scale of 1 to 10, with 10 as the most serious of offenses and 1 as a minor irritation. Numbering the level of offense will not only help you get it in perspective, but sharing the number with the person at whom you are angry may prepare them mentally and emotionally to process the anger with you. If you tell me the issue is a "2," I will know that this will not take all night and that if I give you my full attention and seek to understand, we can solve this one rather easily. On the other hand, if you tell me it is a "10," I know I'm in for a long evening and must postpone my book reading till another night.

FIVE STEPS TO HANDLE VALID ANGER

1. Consciously acknowledge to yourself that you are angry.
2. Restrain your immediate response.
3. Locate the focus of your anger.
4. Analyze your options.
5. Take constructive action.

Locating the focus of your anger and the seriousness of the offense prepares you for taking *step four: Analyze your options.* It is now time to ask the question: What are the possible actions I could take? You may want to write down the thoughts that come to your mind or verbalize them aloud to yourself.

The options are many. You could go back and give them a verbal berating because of their unjust, unkind, unloving, unthinking, uncaring behavior. You could also bring up all the past failures that come to your mind. You could even use curse words to show them how strongly you feel about the matter. You could go back and physically hit them over the head with a ball bat, slap them in the face, shake them vigorously, throw a pop bottle at them. You might dismiss them with a mental put-down: *They're stupid, dumb, ignorant. I'm not going to waste my time even talking about the matter. It doesn't help to talk with an idiot. I'll just go to my computer room and never mention it again.* Or you might try for an element of revenge through isolation: *I will walk out of their lives and never see them again and never give them any further explanation. Let them experience rejection for awhile.* These and many more options may flood your mind.

Which of these, if any, are prudent options? Well, remember our two fundamental questions: Is it positive and is it loving? Does the action I am considering have any potential for dealing with the wrong and helping the relationship? And is it best for the person at whom I am angry? It is my guess you will agree that most of the options we have noted above will not pass these tests. Theoretically they are options, but they are not constructive options. They are the kind of things I may have done in the past, but they are not the kind of things I want to do in the future.

What then are the Christian's options? As I see it, there are only two. One is to lovingly confront the person. The other is to consciously decide to overlook the matter. Let's look at the second option first. There are times when the best Christian option is to admit that I have been wronged but to conclude that confronting the person who did the wrong holds little or no redemptive value. Therefore, I choose to accept the wrong and commit the person to God. This is not the same as stuffing or storing your anger. It is quite the opposite. It is releasing the anger to God. It is giving up the right to take revenge, which, according to Scripture, is always God's prerogative (see Romans 12:19), and it is refusing to let what has happened eat away at your own sense of well-being. You are making a conscious choice to overlook the offense.

This is what the Bible calls forbearance, and it's turning the matter of justice over to God, knowing that He is totally aware of the situation. Thus, God can do to the individual whatever He judges to be wise. You are choosing not to be an emotional captive to the wrong that was perpetrated against you.

At times this option may be the best. For example, your parents have wronged you for many years or hurt you deeply on two or three counts at crucial periods in your life. You have had a surface relationship with them, but the anger has lived in your heart all these years. You have now become a Christian or you are now growing as a Christian, and you want to deal with this anger. You look at your parents who are now in their eighties. You know in your heart that they are not capable of understanding or responding to the hurt which you have felt. You remember making an attempt on one occasion several years ago and getting nowhere. Thus, you decide it's time to let it go.

You may say, "I will never have the in-depth relationship I wish with my parents, but to confront them at this point would be counterproductive; therefore, I release my anger and hurt to God, knowing that He loves me with an unconditional love, knowing that He is both a just and merciful God and will do what is right by my parents." And then you say: "I release my parents to His care, and I release my anger and allow God's Holy Spirit to fill my being and cleanse me from all resentment and anger." You have consciously chosen the road of forbearance.

Here's another instance where a forbearing response might be best. Your supervisor at work has treated you in what you believe is a nonprofessional manner. In fact, he/she has in your opinion treated you unfairly. In the process of analyzing your anger and exploring your options, you remember that five of your friends have confronted the same supervisor within the last three years with what they also thought was unfair treatment. Summarily, each of them was fired and are no longer with the company. Thus you conclude that the supervisor is an uncaring, unreasonable individual, that talking with him/her would likely make things worse. Realizing that you have a family to support and that jobs are not readily available at the moment, you choose to "let it go." You know that choosing to do so will not change your feelings or thoughts about the supervisor. You still feel the hurt and you still perceive that you have been treated unfairly, but you make the conscious choice to let it go. Perhaps you begin looking for another job or perhaps you will realize that to stay with the company means that you will likely not advance up the corporate ladder as long as your supervisor is with the company. In either case, you affirm that confronting the supervisor with your anger will again be counterproductive.

When taking such action, you release both the supervisor and your anger to God. To get on with your life, you deem those actions to be best. Doing so will not enhance your relationship with your supervisor, but at least it gives you the freedom to invest your emotional and physical energies in activities that are more productive.

There are many other occasions in which overlooking the offense may be the best option. The Scriptures acknowledge that this is often a valid way to handle one's anger. For example, "A man's wisdom gives him patience; it is his glory to overlook an offense" (Proverbs 19:11). Our anger is released to God. The whole matter is placed in His hands, and we move on with our lives.

However, far more often the wise response to anger is to lovingly confront the person who has wronged you in an effort to seek resolution. "If your brother sins, rebuke him, and if he repents, forgive him. If he sins against you … and says, 'I repent,' forgive him" (Luke 17:3–4). Notice that Jesus is talking about those with whom you have a relationship. He says, "If your *brother* sins … against you." Furthermore, the word translated *to rebuke* means literally "to set a weight upon." Thus, to rebuke is to lay a matter before someone, to clearly bring it to their attention. There are numerous examples of this in the New Testament.

On one occasion Jesus began to teach His disciples that He was going to suffer many things and be rejected by the elders and chief priests and that He would be killed and after three days, He would rise again. The Scriptures record the reaction of one disciple: "Peter took him aside and began to rebuke him" (Mark 8:32). Why did Peter rebuke Jesus? Because in his mind, what Jesus was saying was wrong. *This is not the way you establish a kingdom. And certainly my master is not going to be killed.* Perhaps Peter thought Jesus was depressed, but he certainly didn't agree with what Jesus was saying, so he privately rebuked Him.

In response, "Jesus turned and looked at his disciples." Then "he rebuked Peter. 'Get behind me, Satan!' he said. 'You do not have in mind the things of God, but the things of men'" (Mark 8:33). Jesus knew that Peter misunderstood reality; that in fact he was speaking the words of Satan. In brief, Peter was wrong and Jesus clearly confronted him with his wrong. On another occasion, Jesus rebuked James and John for their hostile attitude toward the unbelieving Samaritans. They suggested, "'Lord, do you want us to call fire down from heaven to destroy them?' But Jesus turned and rebuked them, and they went to another village" (Luke 9:54–56). Clearly their attitude was wrong, and Jesus brought the matter to their attention.

Rebuke is not verbal abuse. Rebuke is laying a matter before a brother whom you perceive to have wronged you. Such a rebuke needs to be done kindly and firmly, recognizing that there is always a possibility that we have misunderstood the brother's words or actions as Peter misunderstood the words of Jesus regarding the Savior's approaching death. I often suggest that people write their rebuke before trying to speak it. It may go something like this: "I've got something that has been bothering me. In fact, I guess I would have to say I'm feeling angry. Perhaps I am misunderstanding the situation, but when you have an opportunity, I'd like to talk with you about it."

Such a statement reveals where you are, openly reveals your anger, and requests an opportunity to process it with the person involved. You have acknowledged up front that your perception may be imperfect, but at any rate, you want to get the issue resolved. Few people will not respond with an opportunity to talk about it if you approach them in such a manner. If given the opportunity, then you lay before them your perception of what you heard or saw or think to be true and ask if you are understanding the situation correctly. This gives the person an opportunity to share with you information that you may not be aware of or to explain his motives in what he did or said or to clearly admit to you that what he did was wrong and to ask your forgiveness.

In this context of open communication, each trying to understand the other, the issue will be resolved. Either by his explanation or his confession of wrong, the framework is laid for reconciliation. If the person admits to wrongdoing and expresses a repentant attitude, the clear teaching of Jesus is that we are to forgive the individual.

In Matthew 18, Jesus described how this principle works in the context of the local church. "If your brother sins against you, go and show him his fault, just between the two of you. If he listens to you, you have won your brother over. But if he will not listen, take one or two others along, so that 'every matter may be established by the testimony of two or three witnesses.' If he refuses to listen to them, tell it to the church; and if he refuses to listen even to the church, treat him as you would a pagan or a tax collector" (Matthew 18:15–17). And how do you treat a pagan or a tax collector? You pray for his salvation, you pray for his restoration. You treat the person with dignity and respect, as an individual for whom Christ died. But you cannot have warm fellowship with him because he refuses to deal with the offense, which always divides.

Thus, in the church or out of the church, reconciliation with a friend or family member is always the ideal. Confronting is never for the purpose of condemning but rather for restoring the relationship to one that is genuine, open, and loving. If there has been a misunderstanding, the air is to be cleared so that we can go on fellowshiping as brothers or husband and wife. If wrongdoing is confessed, we are to forgive and the relationship is restored. The apostle Paul wrote that we must always remember that we may be the one next time who offends (Galatians 6:1). None of us is perfect and when we do wrong, we are likely to stimulate anger in the person whom we have wronged.

Loving confrontation is not easy for most people. We have had no training and very little experience in this approach to handling anger. We are far more experienced in either ventilating or seeking to deny or hide our anger, but such approaches are always destructive. Loving confrontation with a view to reconciliation is normally the best approach.

FIVE STEPS TO HANDLE VALID ANGER

1. Consciously acknowledge to yourself that you are angry.
2. Restrain your immediate response.
3. Locate the focus of your anger.
4. Analyze your options.
5. Take constructive action.

Which brings us to our *fifth step: Take constructive action.* Once we have explored our options, it is time to take action. If I choose to "let the offense go," then I should share this decision with God. You might say something like this; "Lord, You know what has happened. You know how hurt I am, how angry I feel. But I really believe that the best thing for me to do in this situation is to accept the wrong and turn the person over to You. You know not only his actions but his motives. I know that You are a righteous God, so I trust You to do what is right by the person. I also release my anger to You. The anger stimulated me to think through the situation, and I am taking the step I believe to be best. Therefore, the matter is over. My anger has served its purpose, and I release it to You. Help me not to be controlled by any residual thoughts and feelings that come to me over the next few days. I want to use my life constructively and not be hindered by this event. Thank You that I am Your child and You will take care of me."

If over the next few days or weeks your mind reverts to the wrong done to you and the emotions of hurt and anger return, take those thoughts and feelings to God and say, "Lord, You know what I am remembering right now, and You know the feelings that I am feeling. But I thank You that I have dealt with that and I release these thoughts and feelings to You. Help me now to do something constructive with my life the rest of this day." Then you move out to face the challenges of today.

On the other hand, if you choose the option of lovingly confronting the person who has wronged you, remember the challenge given by Paul. "Brothers, if someone is caught in a sin, you who are spiritual should restore him gently. But watch yourself, or you also may be tempted" (Galatians 6:1). Your confrontation may go something like this: "I have something that is bothering me, and I need your input. Is there a time we can talk?"

If your request is granted, you may say something like, "I'm feeling some hurt and anger over something that happened. I know that I may be misunderstanding the situation. That's why I want to talk about it. Yesterday when you . . . , I interpreted that as a very unkind action. I felt like you were not considering my feelings at all. Maybe I misunderstood your actions, but I need to resolve this." Perhaps the person will give an explanation that will shed light upon his or her actions and give you a different perspective on the actions and the person's intentions. On the other hand, the person may admit that what he or she did was unthoughtful and unkind and may ask you to forgive him or her. In this case, you must always forgive.

If the offense was extremely grave in nature, forgiveness may not restore your trust in the person. We will discuss the nature of forgiveness in a later chapter, but forgiveness is the promise that you will no longer hold this particular offense against the person. Your anger has served its purpose, and the two of you are reconciled.

Such loving confrontation typically results in either a genuine confession of wrongdoing and the extending of forgiveness, or the conversation sheds new light upon the subject; you learn that what the person said or did was not exactly what you had perceived or that the motives were not the ones that you had attributed to them. In either case, the issue is cleared; the matter is resolved and the relationship continues to grow. Anger has served its rightful purpose. It has motivated you to take constructive action to see that the issue was resolved.

FINDING A RESTORED RELATIONSHIP

Confrontation does not always lead to justice, but hopefully it will lead to a restored relationship. Bill, a hard worker, had achieved some success in his business and had accumulated a substantial investment portfolio. Jerry, his longtime friend, was starting a new business and came to Bill asking for a loan of $50,000 to help him get his business off the ground. Bill freely loaned him the money. They each signed a simple loan agreement that he could have the money one year without interest and after that would repay the entire sum or renegotiate the loan.

By the end of the year, Jerry's business was no longer in existence, and the $50,000 had been spent. Jerry got another job, but his salary was not adequate to repay the loan. He promised to repay Bill whenever he was able over the next five years. Jerry never made enough to repay the loan. He had good intentions but never came through with the money. Bill let it ride but struggled with anger toward Jerry.

Bill had a reverse in his own business and could really use the $50,000, but Jerry was not able to pay. After much prayer and talking with his pastor, Bill confronted Jerry and shared his anger. Jerry expressed his own pain that he had not been able to repay the loan. "If I had the money, I would give it to you," he said. "If I ever get it, I will give it to you." Bill decided to no longer expect the money from Jerry. He told Jerry, "We have been friends for a long time. I don't want money to be a barrier between us. If you are ever able to repay the loan, I would really like that, but if not, I'm not going to pressure you over the money."

Bill had the legal right to sue Jerry for failure to repay. However, he knew that to do so would devastate Jerry financially. He chose not to do that, believing that it would serve no good purpose. His was the choice to accept less than he desired. He and Jerry are still friends, and Jerry sincerely hopes that someday he will be able to repay Bill. He is deeply grateful for Bill's attitude. Bill's choice to not press the matter has made it possible for their friendship to endure.

There are times when choosing not to seek justice is the best alternative. For Bill, this was a conscious choice which came after confronting Jerry with his thoughts and feelings. Confrontation led to a resolution that was something less than ideal. But Bill is now free from his anger, and his relationship with Jerry has improved. Loving confrontation always opens up the possibility of dealing with the wrong and restoring the relationship.

Of course, there is always the possibility that when you confront someone the person will deny wrongdoing, even though you know the person has wronged you. This often happens when a spouse confronts a partner who is guilty of having an affair. The partner lies in order to protect himself (herself). The lie itself gives rise to more anger. If you are certain of your facts, you must then realize that you cannot reconcile with this person. Unconfessed sin fractures relations with people and God. You must then decide what your next step will be. This may be turning to a pastor, counselor, or trusted friend to seek advice. It may be reading an appropriate book. It will certainly mean prayer for God's guidance in what you should do.

If after further confrontation the person refuses to deal with his wrongdoing, you must eventually acknowledge the person is choosing not to continue his relationship with you. We cannot make people confess, repent, and reconcile with us. We must let them walk away, and we must pray for them as we would pray for a pagan. Loving confrontation does not always result in reconciliation, but it does give us the peace of mind that we sought to deal with the wrong in a responsible manner.

In summary, here are the steps in responding to anger:

1. Consciously acknowledge to yourself that you are angry.
2. Restrain your immediate response.
3. Locate the focus of your anger.
4. Analyze your options.
5. Take constructive action.

This is the road to making anger productive.

HOW TO HANDLE YOUR ANGER

We can process our anger in a productive manner. Here are the five steps for moving from anger to positive, loving action.

First, consciously acknowledge to yourself that you are angry. Say the words out loud. "I am angry about this! Now what am I going to do?" Such a statement makes you aware of your own anger and also helps you recognize both your anger and the action you are going to take. You have set the stage for applying reason to your anger.

Second, restrain your immediate response. Avoid the common but destructive responses: (1) verbal or physical venting; or their opposite, (2) withdrawal and silence. Refuse to take the action that you typically take when feeling angry. Waiting can both help you avoid saying and doing things you may not mean and later will regret.

Third, locate the focus of your anger. What words or actions by the other person have made you experience anger? Whatever the cause of your anger, locate it. If the person has truly wronged you, identify the person's sin. How has she wronged you? Then determine how serious the offense is. Some wrongs are minor and some are major. Knowing its seriousness should affect your response.

Fourth, analyze your options. Significantly, the response should be positive and loving. Ask yourself, *Does the action I am considering have any potential for dealing with the wrong and helping the relationship? And is it best for the person at whom I am angry?* The two most constructive options are (1) lovingly confront the person and (2) consciously decide to overlook the matter.

Fifth, take constructive action. If you choose to "let the offense go," then express this decision to God. In prayer, confess your anger and your willingness to turn the person over to the righteous and just God. Then release your anger to Him. If you choose to lovingly confront the person who has wronged you, do so gently. Listen to any explanation; it can give you a different perspective on the person's actions and intentions. If the person admits that what he or she did was wrong and asks you to forgive, do so.

FOR DISCUSSION

1. Proverbs 14:17 says, "A quick-tempered man does foolish things." This simple but powerful pearl of wisdom tells us that anger, no matter how justified, can lead to destructive ends if pursued rashly. Relate an experience to your group where you acted too quickly in response to anger. What was the result? What was the negative fallout from your quick-tempered reaction? Compare your response with others.

2. Review the five steps to control and process anger shown above. Explain how you would utilize these steps in helping a coworker experiencing anger over being bypassed for promotion at work. If you can recall a specific experience with such a coworker, add details to assist you and others in thoroughly understanding the process.

3. Turning our anger over to God is a difficult assignment, since we often feel that we must respond to the injustice done to us. Talk through the benefits of turning our anger over to God. How does this make your anger productive? How can you profit when God is given the charge for righting an injustice against you? How can God work within you when you are at fault in a situation? Share experiences with your group. What are the common threads of experience within the group?

4. *Processing your anger:* Your sister and you decide to plan a fortieth wedding anniversary for your parents. Plans include a party for approximately seventy family members and friends, followed by a Caribbean cruise for your parents. Your sister, who lives several hundred miles away from your parents and you, has agreed to share evenly in the party costs. A week before the party, and after most bills have been paid in full by you, your sister calls to announce that she is in a bad financial position. "I'm sorry, but I won't be able to pay my portion of the party and trip expenses." Your parents are aware of the party but not of your sister's financial troubles. In addition to the financial crisis you now face and the awkwardness of canceling at the last minute, you feel betrayed by your sister. Using the five steps for processing anger, explain how you would react in this situation.

Chapter 4

WHEN
ANGER IS
DISTORTED

By this time you may be asking, "If anger is so positive, then why has it caused so much trouble in the world?" The answer is as ancient as the Garden of Eden. The drama revealed in Genesis 3 involving Adam and Eve, the serpent, and a fruit tree significantly changed man's nature. Whatever one's view of the human Fall, subsequent history affirms that the propensity to sin is a part of our nature. God's image is marred in the human clay. The face of God mirrored in the face of man is now distorted. Left to themselves, men and women tend toward doing wrong. We now have the tendency to take every good gift of God and distort it into something perverse. The gifts of reason, sexuality, love, etc., have all been perverted.

Anger is no different. The deceiver is still among us, and the scene of Eden is repeated daily. Perverting the divine purpose of anger has been one of Satan's most successful tactical designs.

The Enemy has used many strategies to mischannel God's intention for human anger. One of the most powerful is to make us think that all of our anger is of equal value; that is, that all of our anger is valid. "If I perceive that I have been wronged, then I have been wronged." This illusion leads us to conclude that whenever we experience anger, we "have a right to be angry."

UNDERSTANDING DISTORTED ANGER

The fact is that much of our anger is distorted. Two kinds of anger exist: definitive and distorted. Definitive anger is born of wrongdoing. Someone treats us unfairly, steals our property, lies about our character, or in some other way does us wrong. This is the only kind of anger God ever experiences, definitive anger. It is valid anger. The second kind of anger, however, is not valid. It is triggered by a mere disappointment, an unfulfilled desire, a frustrated effort, or any number of other things that have nothing to do with any moral transgression. The situation simply has made life inconvenient for us, touched one of our emotional hot spots, or happened at a time when we were extremely tired or stressed.

I call this "distorted anger," not because the emotions are any less intense than those experienced with definitive anger, but because they are the responses to something less than genuine wrongdoing. Most of our anger with inanimate objects is distorted anger. The lawn mower did us no wrong. There is a mechanical explanation for why it will not start, but the lawn mower is not seeking to do us evil. The same is true with a flat tire, a wrench that keeps slipping off the bolt, a gas pilot light that refuses to ignite, etc. These experiences stimulate within us frustration and usually anger as well, but these inanimate objects did not choose to do us wrong.

Much of our anger with people is also distorted. What the person did frustrated me, disappointed me, hurt me, embarrassed me, but what the person did was not actually wrong. My anger experience may be just as intense as ever, but my response to such anger will be different from my response to definitive anger.

BIBLICAL EXAMPLES OF DISTORTED ANGER

Perhaps we can best understand this by looking at some biblical examples. Very early in Genesis we meet Cain, one of the sons of Adam and Eve. He worked in the fields as a farmer, while his brother, Abel, was a shepherd. In due time, they each brought an offering to the Lord—Abel a sheep and Cain some of the "fruits of the soil." According to Genesis 4:4–5, "The Lord looked with favor on Abel and his offering, but on Cain and his offering he did not look with favor. So Cain was very angry, and his face was downcast." A cursory reading may lead us to conclude that Cain had a right to be angry. Why would God reject his offering and accept that of Abel? Apparently, God had made it clear that they were each to bring an animal sacrifice. The importance of this is clear when we understand the rest of Scripture and the central role of the sacrificial lamb, Jesus, who is God's only plan of redemption. However, Cain decided to do it his way, which is at the center of all sin. "Why wouldn't vegetables be just as good?" he must have reasoned.

When we place human reason above God's clear commands, we have made a serious misjudgment. Cain followed his reason, offered his sacrifice, and experienced God's rejection. Then he blamed God with being unfair. God's response to Cain was straightforward. "Then the Lord said to Cain, 'Why are you angry? Why is your face downcast? If you do what is right, will you not be accepted? But if you do not do what is right, sin is crouching at your door; it desires to have you, but you must master it'" (verses 6–7).

Cain's anger toward God was not legitimate. It was not based upon God's wrongdoing but rather upon Cain's perception of wrongdoing.

His experience of rejection and anger were real, but they were distorted. God's challenge was for Cain to deal with his own wrongdoing, release his anger, and come back into warm fellowship with God. However, Cain did not respond to God's overture. The next verse records that he invited his brother Abel to take a walk out to his fields. There Cain killed Abel. In so doing, he became the first of many who allowed distorted anger to control behavior and thus end up compounding their problems. The course of human history would have been much different if Cain had acknowledged that his anger was distorted, released it to God, repented of his own sin, and got on with his farming.

Another example is Jonah. You will remember that after Jonah's tumultuous sea voyage, he had made his way to Nineveh and proclaimed the clear message that God had given him: "Forty more days and Nineveh will be overturned" (Jonah 3:4). Much to Jonah's dismay, the people believed his message, declared a fast, and repented of their wrong deeds. Even the king took off his royal robes and covered himself with sackcloth and sat down in the dust. He called upon the people to pray and turn from their evil ways in hopes that God would forgive and turn from His intentions. In keeping with His character, God had compassion and did not bring destruction upon the city.

When Jonah learned of this change of events, the Scriptures say he was "greatly displeased and became angry. He prayed to the Lord, 'O Lord, is this not what I said when I was still at home? That is why I was so quick to flee to Tarshish. I knew that you are a gracious and compassionate God, slow to anger and abounding in love, a God who relents from sending calamity. Now, O Lord, take away my life, for it is better for me to die than to live'" (4:1–3). Jonah was greatly embarrassed. He had proclaimed a message that now appeared to be untrue. *Why did God do this to me—interrupted my life in order to embarrass me? God knew that the people would repent. He has made me look like a fool. I'd rather die than live.* These must have been the thoughts that raced through the mind of Jonah.

However, Jonah's anger was distorted. Listen to the words of Scripture: "The Lord replied, 'Have you any right to be angry?'" (4:4). Jonah did not respond to God's question. Rather he walked outside the city, made himself a shelter, sat in its shade, and waited to see what would happen. God cooperated in making his shelter more comfortable by causing a quick-growing vine to give Jonah further shade. This pleased Jonah, but in the morning God sent a worm to eat the vine and it withered. Jonah was more angry than ever. Again, God said to Jonah, "Do you have a right to be angry about the vine?" And now Jonah started talking. "'I do,' he said. 'I am angry enough to die.' But the Lord said, 'You have been concerned about this vine, though you did not tend it or make it grow. It sprang up overnight and died overnight. But Nineveh has more than a hundred and twenty thousand people who cannot tell their right hand from their left, and many cattle as well. Should I not be concerned about that great city?'" (verses 9–11).

Jonah's anger was illegitimate. It grew out of his own distorted thinking. He was focusing on himself and his reputation. He was relying on human reason rather than responding to truth. God had done him no wrong. In fact, had Jonah listened to God, he would have realized that he was privileged to be a part of the good work God did in Nineveh. Rather than being embarrassed, he would have had the pleasure of being honored.

Jonah allowed his distorted anger to control his disposition and to lead him to the brink of suicide. The Scriptures do not tell where Jonah went from there. We can only hope that he listened to the word of the Lord, realized that his anger was based on faulty thinking, not upon any wrongdoing on God's part; that he would have released his anger, congratulated the king of Nineveh on his response, prayed for the city of Nineveh, and returned home a faithful messenger of God.

That people can recognize when anger is distorted and make positive responses is illustrated by the story of Naaman, a great military commander and valiant soldier who had leprosy. The commander had heard from a young girl, a prisoner of war, that a prophet in Israel could heal leprosy. Naaman immediately went to the king, told him what the young girl had said, and asked permission to go to the prophet in Israel. The king not only gave permission but encouraged Naaman in his pursuit. Naaman packed his gold, silver, and other gifts and headed off in search of healing. When through a circuitous route he finally reached the gate that led to the prophet's house, the prophet did not so much as go to the door. Rather he sent a messenger, saying to Naaman,

> *"Go, wash yourself seven times in the Jordan, and your flesh will be restored and you will be cleansed." But Naaman went away angry and said, "I thought that he would surely come out to me and stand and call on the name of the Lord his God, wave his hand over the spot and cure me of my leprosy. Are not Abana and Pharpar, the rivers of Damascus, better than any of the waters of Israel? Couldn't I wash in them and be cleansed?" So he turned and went off in a rage.*
>
> —2 Kings 5:10–12

Clearly, Naaman is an angry man. His blood pressure has risen. His nostrils are flared. His feet are stamping the dry ground. His anger quickly jumps to rage. Thoughts, which to him seem logical, race through his mind. *How absurd, how foolish. Where is the respect? I'm giving him a chance to show his God's power, and he tells me to go wash in the muddy Jordan. How ridiculous.* In Naaman's mind, Elisha the prophet has done him wrong. He has a right to be angry. Instead, the prophet has actually given him a cure for his leprosy. Elisha has done him great good, but because Naaman's thinking is distorted, he is experiencing anger toward the prophet. In his rage, he is ready to return to his homeland, his mission not only a failure but a great embarrassment.

Fortunately, there were some straight-thinking people traveling with him. His servants went to him and said,

> *"My father, if the prophet had told you to do some great thing, would you not have done it? How much more, then, when he tells you, 'Wash and be*

cleansed'!" So he went down and dipped himself in the Jordan seven times, as the man of God had told him, and his flesh was restored and became clean like that of a young boy. Then Naaman and all his attendants went back to the man of God. He stood before him and said, "Now I know that there is no God in all the world except in Israel. Please accept now a gift from your servant."

—*verses 13–15*

Elisha refused his gift but acknowledged the healing power of God.

Naaman represents the person who experiences strong but distorted anger but who, when confronted, stops his rage and listens to reason rather than allow anger to control his behavior. As a result, this leader experienced healing and turned to honor the person at whom he had earlier been angry. Naaman demonstrates that distorted anger does not need to control our behavior and lead us to destructive acts.

These biblical accounts give us both negative and positive examples of how to respond to distorted anger. This raises two questions: (1) How do we identify when our anger is distorted? (2) How do we process distorted anger? The first question is easier to answer, and we'll address it here. However, processing distorted anger is more challenging, and we'll answer that in the next chapter.

IDENTIFYING DISTORTED ANGER

Distorted anger differs from definitive anger in one fundamental way. In definitive anger, there is always a wrong perpetrated; the anger is a response to this wrong. In distorted anger, a perceived wrong leads to anger—but the alleged wrong is only in your perception; there is no real wrongdoing.

For instance, you are walking down the street and observe an older teenage boy walk up to a younger and smaller boy, snatch his bicycle from his grip, and ride off down the street. The young boy is screaming, "That's my bike! That's my bike! He stole my bike!" Immediately you experience anger. Your emotions rise. The biological characteristics of anger set in. Your thoughts are stimulated. *The very idea of bullying around a younger child.* Your mind is saying, *That's not right. Something needs to be done.* If the facts are what you perceive them to be, then your anger is definitive.

But let's assume that upon further investigation, you find that the bicycle actually belonged to the older boy, that the younger boy saw it unattended

and decided to take a ride. When the older boy spotted him, he was simply re-
trieving his bicycle before the young boy got out of sight. Your anger toward
the older boy is distorted in that he perpetrated no wrong. In fact, he was correcting a wrong that had been committed by the younger boy. Distorted
anger is based upon a perception of wrong, whereas definitive anger is based
upon genuine wrong.

It becomes apparent that if we treat all anger as definitive, we will make
some serious blunders in judgment. For example, if in the above illustration,
you assume that your anger is definitive you may chase the older teen, knock
him from the bicycle, and return it to the younger child. Only later will you
realize that you have made a serious mistake.

In order to understand distorted anger, we must return to our basic paradigm. In all anger there is first a stimulating event; second, an interpretation
of that event; third, the emotion of anger arises. Physiological changes take
place in the body, and we are ready for action. All of this occurs whether the
anger is definitive or distorted. But if we are to have a wise response to anger,
we must first discern whether that anger is based upon actual wrongdoing.
This requires time and thought. Thus, the value of step two in the last chapter: Restrain your immediate response. Restraining your immediate response gives you the opportunity to question the validity of your anger.
Questions must be asked and evidence must be weighed in order to process
anger positively. These questions must be asked of yourself and sometimes of
the other person.

In the illustration above, had you raced to the younger child and asked,
"Is that your bicycle?" he may have said, "No, I was just borrowing it for a
short ride." Immediately you know that things are not exactly what you perceive them to be. With only one bit of new information, your anger is already
beginning to subside. As you ask further questions of both boys and get a
better picture, your anger toward the older boy goes away or at least lessens.
With the additional information, you may decide that no action toward the
older boy needs to be taken, and you may end up giving the younger boy a
lecture on not taking bicycles without permission; that's a much different action than you would have taken if you assumed your original anger to be definitive. (Of course, if you heard different stories from the two boys, any
action is difficult. You may assume one is lying. The solution may be to go
home with one of the boys and talk with his parents.)

Two questions are important in determining the validity of anger. The first is, "What wrong was committed?" And the second is, "Am I sure I have all the facts?" The first question strikes at the heart of the matter. If a genuine wrong has been committed, then your anger is definitive. If, however, your anger has been born out of some unrealistic expectation inside of you, then it must be handled as distorted anger. Much of our anger grows out of internal emotional and thinking patterns that have developed through the years. For example, the person who tends to be perfectionistic will have high expectations not only for himself but for others to whom he relates. When people do not live up to these expectations, he will likely experience anger. Such anger is often distorted anger because the person has committed no wrong.

Jill is highly perfectionistic. Open the drawer of her dresser and you find all of her clothes neatly stacked and color-coordinated. Her closet is no less organized. This pattern for neatness and perfection appears in every aspect of her life. She is married to Jeff, who is highly creative, but neatness and organization are not even in his vocabulary. Jill often becomes angry when she observes Jeff's dirty clothes stuffed in a closet corner; when she sees him looking for a report he completed two weeks ago but has misplaced; and when she gets inside his car, which hasn't been cleaned since the day he brought it home from the dealer. If you happen to identify with Jill, I do not wish to stimulate your anger toward me, yet I do wish to suggest that Jill's anger is distorted.

Jeff has committed no wrong; Jeff is being the person Jeff has learned to be. He has no inner compulsion toward neatness or organization such as Jill has. I am not suggesting that Jill's anger is not real. It has the same emotional, physical, and cognitive aspects as definitive anger. She really is upset; she really believes that Jeff is wrong not to be neat. But if she is open to the facts, she will discover that thousands of people have Jeff's personality traits and that these traits are not evil. Jill's anger still needs to be processed in a positive way (we'll come to that in the next chapter), but it will help if she can see it for what it is. Her anger is not born out of Jeff's wrongdoing but out of her own compulsion for neatness and organization. If she can see it as distorted anger, she is far more likely to process it in a positive way.

Sometimes examining our anger will lead us to question the person with whom we are angry. If we understand that we may not have all the facts, then we should be motivated to seek the facts before we jump to wrong conclusions. Patrick experiences anger when he walks in the door and sees his shirts lying on the chair where he left them this morning. Why is he angry? Because Beth had told him that she would be happy to drop his shirts by the laundry if he would just put them on the chair. He needs one of the shirts for tomorrow. He anticipated picking them up from the laundry after dinner; now there is no chance that he will have a clean shirt tomorrow.

In his mind, many thoughts are racing. *How could she be so irresponsible? I can't depend on her for anything. She doesn't love me. If she loved me, she would not let things like this happen.* He may even accuse her of being selfish. *She only thinks of herself.* By the time Beth walks in the door, Patrick is halfway to the divorce court in his mind. He glances at her and sarcastically says, "Thanks for all your help."

"What help, Sweetheart?" she says.

"My shirts. You were supposed to take them to the laundry. I need one tomorrow. Now I guess I will wear dirty shirts to work."

"Oh, Darling," she says. "I'm so sorry. I forgot. I was in a rush this morning and I simply forgot."

What happens from there is probably a saga that has been played out many evenings in their home. It may be an evening of withdrawal and silent misery and rejection in which Beth puts herself down for being so forgetful, and he puts her down for the same reason. It may be an evening of verbal tirades in which both of them point out the other's past failures. If either of these patterns is true, they need to be changed. We'll talk about changing destructive patterns in chapter 6; our question here is the validity of Patrick's anger.

Again, at the risk of stimulating anger inside of the men who identify with Patrick, I want to suggest that Patrick's anger is distorted anger. The question is, "Did Beth commit a wrong?" The answer is clearly no. I know that some of you are screaming, "But she promised and she broke her promise." I'm asking, "Was that a conscious choice?" The answer is no. She simply forgot. Forgetting is a human phenomenon. It is not a sin. Who has not forgotten something they fully intended to do, either for themselves or for a family member? The fact is, we are forgetful creatures. A mind that can remember can also forget.

Does her forgetting place an inconvenience on Patrick? Yes. Is his anger real? Yes. Along with his anger, does he feel frustration, disappointment, and perhaps a whole cluster of other emotions? Yes. And all of those emotions need to be processed in a positive way.

The first step is acknowledging that his anger is distorted; that Beth has not intentionally wronged him, even though her forgetfulness obviously frustrates him. But if he blames her for being human, it is only a matter of time before he must also turn the blame to himself, for sooner or later he will also forget.

When we begin to examine anger, we will find that much of it falls into the category of distorted anger. Distorted anger is no less troublesome than definitive anger, but it needs to be processed in a different way. In chapter 5 we will consider how to process our distorted anger.

DEFINITIVE VERSUS DISTORTED ANGER

*R*ecognizing distorted anger and dealing with it is crucial, for while definitive anger is valid, distorted anger is not and must be handled differently. The differences between definitive and distorted anger are more than just in definitions. The following chart shows several ways the two kinds of anger differ.

	DEFINITIVE ANGER	DISTORTED ANGER
Definition	Anger toward any kind of genuine wrongdoing: mistreatment, injustice, breaking of laws	Anger toward a perceived wrongdoing; the perception is inaccurate—no wrong-doing occurred
Common Sources	Violation of laws or moral codes	Inanimate object (such as flat tire), people who hurt or embarrass us, stress, tiredness, unrealistic expectations
Ways to Recognize	Be able to answer yes to two questions: (1) Was a wrong committed? (2) Do I definitely have all the facts?	Feelings of frustration or disappointment are spurring the anger
Proper Responses	Either lovingly confront the person or decide to overlook the offense. (See chapter 3, "Step Four: Analyze Your Options.")	Halt the anger, and gather information to process your anger. Naaman illustrates the right response. (The formal four-step process is detailed in chapter 5.)

FOR DISCUSSION

1. Much of our anger is distorted. We experience feelings of genuine anger, but the reason for the anger or its cause is misunderstood by us. We may feel anger at a friend for not sending us a Christmas card, when in fact the friend has been ill and unable to keep up with normal holiday correspondence. Identify a time in your past when you wrongly attributed an injustice to someone. How did you determine that this was distorted anger? Who or what was really the source of the anger? How was the anger resolved?

2. With distorted anger, unlike definitive anger, the wrongdoing is perceived, not genuine. To be able to successfully identify anger as being distorted, we must restrain our initial tendency to react to the perceived wrong and stop to analyze the situation. We must be willing to inquire among the party(s) concerned to arrive at the source of our anger. Recall some experience of distorted anger. How did you determine that their (or your) anger was distorted? Did you determine this in time to positively settle the situation and process the anger constructively? Or did the revelation of distortion come much later, after some relational damage had already been done? Share experiences within your group.

3. During the Exodus from Egypt, Moses acted as the Lord's agent in revealing His will to the Israelites. Very often, Moses' anger mirrored God's anger. Review Exodus to determine if Moses ever demonstrated distorted anger. If you locate such an instance, what was it? What were the effects of his distorted anger?

4. *Processing your anger:* You are the manager of a fast-food restaurant. You normally close the restaurant yourself at 10:00 P.M., but you have to leave early to handle a minor crisis at home. You tell your assistant to "take care of things" and to close at 10 o'clock. When you come in the next morning, you discover the doors to the restaurant are not locked and that someone has come in and stolen various items. Although you forgot to give your assistant the keys, there is another set of keys in your office in the back room. You are angry at your assistant for causing the situation. Is your anger definitive or distorted? How can you find out? What factors would make it distorted? Definitive?

Chapter 5

PROCESSING
DISTORTED
ANGER

*A*ll of us have had distorted anger based on a perceived injustice that never really happened. We can develop such anger in many ways: circumstantial evidence, faulty presuppositions, generalizations, our expectations or personal preferences, even plain tiredness—and sometimes a combination of these factors. Whatever the cause, we conclude incorrectly that we have been wronged. We have an anger that is not valid, definitive anger, but mistaken, distorted anger.

The mother is angry her daughter receives a D in history, a subject Mom enjoyed greatly in school. (It was her college major.) A secretary finds herself depressed and angry by the petty criticism and gossip by other secretaries about the company. The husband fumes that his wife left his shirts lying on the chair instead of taking them to the cleaners, as he expected her to do. The last case, of course, is Patrick being upset over Beth's inaction. Yet the mother, the secretary, and Patrick all must deal with what is actually distorted anger.

We have emphasized that distorted anger is wrong, and that it is a direct outcome of the Fall, rising out of our selfish, even prideful natures. But that does not rid us of our feelings as we are experiencing anger. So how do we address such anger? What do we do to process distorted anger, channeling it for the good?

Since much of our anger is distorted anger, it is extremely important that we learn how to process it positively. There are three essential elements in constructively processing distorted anger, often accompanied by a fourth.

SHARING INFORMATION

We begin by telling the other person our point of concern. This must always be done in a nonjudgmental manner. That's why I am calling it "sharing information." We are not sharing a verdict: "You let me down"; "You disappointed me"; "You didn't do what you promised." All of these are condemning, judgmental statements that tend to stimulate warfare. In contrast, "I'm feeling frustrated (disappointed, hurt, angry, or any other emotion), and I need your help" is a statement of information. It's telling the other person what's going on inside of you, and it is requesting an opportunity to talk.

Had Patrick used this approach, he might have said the following to Beth after he had hugged her, assured her of his love, and asked about her day. "Sweetie, I'm frustrated because when I walked in I saw my dirty shirts still lying on the chair, and I don't have any clean shirts for tomorrow." He is giving her information about his feelings, his shirts, and his prospects for tomorrow. Since his comments are nonjudgmental, Beth may very well say, "Oh, Patrick. I am *so* sorry. I forgot to take them to the laundry. I was in a rush and simply walked out and forgot to take them. Don't worry, Darling. I'll wash your shirt and iron it tonight. You'll have a clean shirt for tomorrow." Or she may volunteer to take it to the hour laundry which is open till midnight. She didn't feel put down or condemned; therefore, she was free to acknowledge her forgetfulness and seek to deal with the immediate issue of getting him a shirt for the next day.

Sharing information rather than judgments is the first step in processing distorted anger. In sharing information, you are focusing on making the other person aware of your emotions, your thoughts, and your concerns. You are focusing on the event that stimulated your feelings, not on the person. You are more likely to be able to do this if you have first determined that your anger is distorted; that is, the person has not wronged you. He may have made your life difficult, he may have caused you frustration, but he has not committed an immoral act.

GATHERING INFORMATION

The second step is gathering information. Earlier we noted that on some occasions, we will recognize that we don't have all the facts. Therefore, it is difficult for us to determine whether our anger is definitive or not. Meredith and Jason have a quick dinner, and she dashes out the door to attend her aerobics class. Three hours later, she returns home to find Jason on the couch watching television, the dirty dishes still sitting on the table where they left them. Meredith goes into an "anger attack." Thoughts wildly race through her mind. *I can't believe this—watching television two and one-half hours and the plates are still on the table. The ants have probably cleaned them by now. What is he thinking about? He's got football on the brain. I feel like going in there and kicking the television—better yet, kicking him. What a slob. I'm out there working hard trying to keep in shape and he's lying on the couch drinking Pepsi. I feel like going in there and pouring the Pepsi on his head.*

Meredith has several options. She can conclude that her anger is legitimate, that her husband is a no-good, lazy slob; and she can respond to him with bitter words; she can withdraw in silence and be unresponsive to his efforts toward sexual intimacy later that evening; or she can try to handle her anger in a more responsible manner. If she understands the difference between definitive and distorted anger, she may begin by asking herself, "What wrong has he committed?" She may work hard in her mind to see his action (or inaction) as some sin. If she is successful, she may conclude that his sin is in not loving her. *After all, aren't husbands supposed to love their wives as Christ loved the church? Well, this is certainly not an expression of love. If he loved me, washing the dishes is the least he could have done.* So she concludes that his sin is failing to express love to her.

If she is wise, she will also ask the question, "Do I have all the facts?" If she is wise enough to ask the question, she will probably be wise enough to conclude that the answer is "no"; she does not have all the facts. Therefore, an important step is to get information from Jason as to what has happened and why.

Going into the den, Meredith walks over to the couch, sits down, gives Jason a big hug and says, "I have one small question before I give you a kiss. Why are the dirty plates still on the table?"

"Oh, Babe, I'm sorry," Jeff answers. "I sat down here to watch the news. I meant to get the dishes right after the news but then the game started and the next thing I knew, I heard the garage door open. I don't know how long I slept. I don't even remember the halftime. I must have been asleep for two hours.

"I'll get the dishes; I'm sorry. I must have been more tired than I realized." He walks off to the kitchen to begin to clean up the table. "How was your evening?" he says.

Chances are Meredith's anger begins to subside as she realizes that Jason's failure to clean up the table was not a sinful act. Sleeping for two hours on the couch is not immoral; it is simply a sign of one's humanity. Gathering information allowed Meredith to release her anger and perhaps even be glad that Jason was able to get some extra sleep. Gathering information is an important step in determining whether anger is definitive or distorted. When we realize that our perception of the situation is distorted, we can release that distorted anger and work on accepting our spouses as human.

NEGOTIATING UNDERSTANDING

The third step in processing distorted anger constructively is negotiating understanding. Sometimes even when our anger is distorted we cannot simply release it and accept what the spouse has done. Often we need to negotiate understanding. For even when your spouse has done nothing morally wrong, his or her behavior is still painful. You still feel disappointed, frustrated, hurt, and angry. You need to understand your spouse's actions and for your partner to understand your feelings.

This requires open conversation in a nonjudgmental atmosphere. Understanding that your anger is distorted—that is, your spouse has not morally wronged you—should help you approach them in a non-condemning way.

Rita and Doug are in their late thirties. They both have vocations that they find fulfilling. However, Rita has been experiencing a lot of anger toward Doug over the last six months. All of a sudden, he has become health-conscious. Three evenings a week after dinner, he goes to the local gym to work out, leaving her with the dishes and the children. He comes home later and wants her to watch television with him and, to use his words, "make love" with him. She is finding her anger growing into resentment. She doesn't like what she is feeling, and she certainly doesn't like what's happening to Doug. She feels that he is neglecting his responsibilities to help the children with their homework on those three nights. She feels that he is unthoughtful and unloving toward her and that while he expects sex from her, he shows no concern for meeting her needs. Rita's anger is growing daily. She feels like she is about to explode. Doug seems to be happy, but she is extremely unhappy.

When Rita expressed her anger to me in the counseling office, we began by trying to focus on the source of her anger. We tried to identify the specific things about Doug's behavior that stimulated her anger. We came up with the following list:

- Doug is unfair to leave me with the dishes while he goes off to have fun.
- He is neglecting the children by not helping them with their homework on those three nights.
- He is self-centered in that he expresses almost no interest in meeting my needs. In fact, I'm not sure he even understands what my needs are.

When we explored her needs, we found that her primary love language —the way she really felt loved by her husband—was quality time; the thing she really wanted from Doug was time together. "We used to talk a lot," she said. "I felt close to him; I felt like he cared. Now with him gone three nights a week, we just don't have time to talk. I'm beginning to feel he doesn't want to be with me."

We then turned our attention toward determining if her anger was distorted in these three areas. We looked at him leaving her with the dirty dishes three nights a week and I asked, "What wrong is he committing?"

"It just seems unfair," Rita said.

"Do you cook the meals on those three nights?" I inquired.

"Only on one of them," she said. "The other two, we bring in food."

"So on those two nights, the dishes would be minimal? Am I correct in assuming that?" I asked.

"Yes; I guess it's just the principle of the thing. I just feel like it's unfair for him to walk out and leave me with the work. We both work outside the home. I work as hard as he does," she said.

"Does he help you around the house in other ways?" I inquired.

"Yes, actually he does a lot around the house. He takes care of the yard and all the outside work and keeps the cars clean. He also vacuums the floors for me. And he'll pitch in and help me with anything I ask him to do."

Then we turned to the matter of homework. "On the two nights that Doug does not go to the gym, does he help the children with their homework?"

"Yes," she said. "He always has. In fact, he used to help them every night.

He still helps them a little bit when he gets home from the gym if there is something they're having trouble with. But it's not the same as it used to be."

"Are the children doing well in school?" I inquired.

"Yes, they're both good students. That's never been a problem."

"Do you ever help the children with their homework?" I asked.

"Sometimes, but not often. That's always been Doug's responsibility. He seemed to enjoy it up until now."

"What was your life like before Doug started going to the gym three nights a week?"

"We would eat together unless the kids had a school activity, and then we would just grab a bite. He would always help me with the dishes. Then he and I would sit down and talk for probably thirty minutes before he helped the children with their homework and I worked on other things around the house. It was great. I felt close to him. I felt like we were a family. Now I feel like we're still a family but he abandons us three nights a week."

When I asked if her husband knew about her feelings toward his gym nights, she thought not, but then she added, "I feel like he is neglecting me and that we are growing apart.... He just doesn't realize what's happening."

As I questioned Rita further, she explained that Doug began to go to the gym after watching a film at his work on physical fitness and a coworker invited him to work out together. She admitted, "I'm glad he's taking care of himself. I'm sure he feels better. I probably should be working out myself, but I just don't have time. I don't think he has time either, but he's making time. But it's at our expense, as I see it."

It seemed apparent to me that Doug's behavior did not fall into the category of immoral. What he was doing was not innately wrong. However, Rita's anger needed to be processed. In fact, she had held onto it far too long. It was already getting to the beginning stages of resentment. Rita needed to negotiate understanding. She needed to share with Doug what was going on inside of her—her thoughts, her feelings, her frustrations—not in a condemning manner but as information. And she needed to find out from Doug how he perceived these things; she needed to get information. But beyond that, this couple needed to come to a place of understanding, to find a way to meet all of their needs, and to help them reconnect with each other emotionally.

I suggested that Rita request of Doug a time to talk and that she begin by saying something like the following: "I know that you love me and you are a good husband. What I want to share with you is not designed in any way to put you down. But I want our relationship to be open and genuine, and I feel that I must share with you some of the struggles that I'm having. Over the past few months, I've sometimes felt hurt, disappointed, and neglected. A lot of it focuses around you going to the gym three nights a week.

"Please understand that I'm not against your efforts to stay in shape. I'm not even asking you to change that. I just want to share with you my struggles. My feelings focus on three specific areas. One, I feel that the children are being neglected in terms of your helping them with their homework. I know that you still help them at night, but I have a concern that they're not getting all the help they need. Secondly, I feel like it's unfair that you get up from the dinner table and leave me to clean up on those three nights. And probably my biggest struggle is that I feel like I'm being neglected, that we don't have time to talk like we used to talk. Sometimes, I even feel like you don't want to talk with me, and I'm feeling a lot of distance between us. I felt it was unfair not to tell you about this because I need your help and your understanding."

My efforts were to help Rita share her struggles in a non-condemning manner, requesting understanding. That is my recommendation to anyone who, having recognized distorted anger and received information, needs to negotiate understanding. Sit down and express your need for understanding in a nonthreatening way.

Then I encouraged Rita to listen to Doug's response; not to try to counter what he said, but rather to understand what he said. Then together they could seek to discover a way to meet her need for quality time with him, his need for physical fitness, the children's need for help with the homework, and her need for a feeling of equity in household responsibilities.

A month later Rita returned, and I was thrilled to hear that Doug had responded positively. In their conversation, he had assured her of his love; he agreed that together they would ask the children if they felt they were getting enough help with their homework and if not, he was willing to make adjustments. He readily agreed to help her clean up the table before he went to the gym. He had not realized that this was a problem with her, and he agreed that they would make time for the two of them. In fact, for the past few weeks, they had been having lunch together two days a week, and he had arranged for a weekend away just for the two of them. If necessary, he was willing to cut back on his time at the gym, but Rita hesitated to encourage this after she saw Doug's positive response to her concerns.

Negotiating understanding is an important part of human relationships, whether the relationship be in the family, church, vocation, or any other area. All of us feel better about our relationships when we negotiate understanding. Even distorted anger indicates that something needs attention. Such anger seldom dissipates without open, loving communication between the parties involved.

REQUESTING CHANGE

A fourth element in processing distorted anger exists that is often helpful: requesting change. In all human relationships, people will find certain behavioral characteristics irritating. Though the particular behaviors may differ, the resulting irritations often stir anger within us. For the most part, this anger is distorted, in that the other person's behavior is not morally wrong; he or she has not perpetrated an evil against us. If the relationship is a close relationship and the person one with whom we spend a great deal of time, such as in family or vocation, it is sometimes helpful to seek to mitigate these irritations by requesting change. Please notice I say *requesting*, not demanding or manipulating. None of us responds well to those approaches.

If we have a generally positive relationship, however, most of us tend to respond well to requests. For example, here's an irritation that causes you anger in the workplace: Your secretary tends to slurp her coffee while you are talking to a client next door. You hear the slurping through the door and find it to be very offensive. After affirming her worth as a secretary and how much you appreciate all that she does, it is perfectly appropriate to request that she not drink coffee while you are seeing a client or that she learn to drink it silently. Chances are a simple request will alleviate the source of your frustration and anger, especially if you make it clear that you are also open to her requests.

The same principle applies in marriage and family relationships. Assuming a fairly good relationship, most husbands will respond to the wife's request that he wear a sport shirt, not a tee shirt, when he goes to the grocery store, especially if she makes her request after affirming her love for him, telling him how handsome he looks, and assuring him that her motive is that he look his best. Most wives will respond to the request to put their dirty pantyhose in the closet rather than draping them over the bedroom chair if the husband makes his request after pointing out some positive traits about her and expressing his appreciation for all the other things that she does. The bottom line is that in most relationships, assuming we feel loved and respected by the other person, most of us are willing to make changes if they are couched in the form of a request rather than a demand. Such requests and subsequent changes can alleviate many of the irritating behaviors that stimulate anger.

Distorted anger is no less real and fully as disturbing as definitive anger. Both need to be thoroughly processed so that the anger does not build to resentment. The approaches are somewhat different. In my opinion, processing distorted anger is much easier than processing definitive anger. Finding constructive rather than destructive methods of processing both is our objective.

PROCESSING YOUR DISTORTED ANGER

*L*ike definitive anger, distorted anger must be fully processed so that the anger does not build toward resentment. The approach is somewhat different from that for definitive anger, which was outlined in chapter 3. (See "How to Handle Your Anger," page 49.) In both kinds of anger, however, your goal is the same: to find constructive rather than destructive methods of processing the anger.

There are four steps to processing possible distorted anger. *First, share information.* Tell the other person about your concern in a non-condemning way, and request an opportunity to talk about it. Be sure to focus on the event that stimulated your feelings, not on the person.

Second, gather information. When you properly gather the facts, you can determine whether the anger is definitive or actually distorted.

Third, negotiate understanding. Express your struggles in a nonthreatening manner, requesting understanding. Then listen to the other person's response. This two-part process allows you to understand the person's actions and for the other person to understand your feelings. This requires open, honest conversation.

Fourth, request change. This final step is optional, but it can lead to lessening many of the irritating behaviors that stimulate anger. Many people will respond well to such a request, as long as you neither demand nor manipulate for the change. A generally positive relationship with the other person will make them more open to such a request.

FOR DISCUSSION

1. The next step after recognizing distorted anger is processing this anger. Since it is a perception based on erroneous thinking, much of the processing will deal with our ability to recognize and correct our own misperception(s) and adjust our own thinking. This does not, however, remove the sense of anger that we feel about the situation. Chapter 5 gives us three essential elements to properly processing distorted anger. The first element is sharing information. We begin by telling the other person our point of view. Share some experience where you shared information with others in a distorted anger situation. How was the information conveyed? Was it done in anger or calmly? Were all parties receptive to discussing the issue? What conditions must be in place for "information sharing" to work effectively? Why?

2. The second element is gathering information. Using the same example(s) you recalled in question 1, explain how the information-sharing process worked. Did you (or another group member) successfully obtain the cooperation of involved parties? What kinds of information did you seek? Were you looking for answers or looking to affix blame in your search for information?

3. The third step is negotiating understanding. We must negotiate an understanding with that party that acknowledges that we accept the benign intent of their action, but that it has still had a hurtful effect upon us. In this way, we can process our anger constructively, while helping the other party become sensitive to the unintended outcome of their act. Again using your examples from question 1, tell the group how you achieved a negotiated understanding with the party(s) involved. Did the other party respond sympathetically? How did that person's response aid or hinder your anger resolution?

4. *Processing your anger:* You are a carpenter who comes from a long line of carpenters going back four generations. This lineage has always been a source of pride in your family. Your only child, now a senior in high school, announces that he wants to go to college and major in philosophy. He tells you that he has no desire to be a carpenter. Although you never insisted that he become a carpenter, you always assumed that he would follow in the family tradition. This sudden announcement has made you furious. Is this definitive or distorted anger? How will you resolve this situation positively?

Chapter 6

DESTRUCTIVE RESPONSES TO ANGER

*T*he flame shot upward, fueled by a break in a city gas line. The line had ruptured when a private contractor, clearing land, clipped a gas pipe. At first just the pressurized gas poured out, hissing loudly. But within thirty minutes, a random spark had ignited the natural gas, which flamed skyward.

Within minutes the fiery plume was almost five stories high, and only a few yards away from Chicago public housing that lodged senior citizens. Fortunately, police and others evacuated the residents from the building. But when the gas company finally stopped the fuel feeding the line, scores of people had been displaced, their housing gutted or scorched.

Two months later, in December 1998, another explosion would displace Chicago residents. This time, though, the explosion was planned. A series of dynamite charges rigged by a demolition company popped in succession, and, one by one, four adjoining buildings at a different public housing project fell, crumbling to the ground and raising huge clouds of dust.

The differences were this explosion was actually an implosion, with building materials falling inward; and the destruction had been planned for months, as the run-down housing would be replaced with various scattered housing. In fact, former residents and other spectators watched a safe distance away, some oohing and aahing, and many even applauding.

Which do you think was the more destructive event? Was it the gas-line explosion that charred the side of a building and left people without homes? Many would say yes, for this devastation was unplanned and people had no alternative housing. In the case of the demolished public housing, most of the displaced residents already had arranged for replacement housing.

In truth, both the gas explosion and the building implosion had equally destructive consequences. In fact, with the implosion, more buildings fell, greater dust and debris gathered, and many of the former residents regretted leaving the apartment housing that for years they had called home. Their emotional loss and personal pain were no less.

Similarly, there are two equally devastating responses to anger: explosion and implosion. We may think that one is more destructive than the other, but the truth is implosive anger can be as damaging as explosive expressions of anger. Both can occur at varying levels of intensity, yet either response has destructive consequences. They represent destructive ways of responding to anger.

We have looked at constructive ways of responding to anger in the last three chapters, but let's be honest, many of us have never learned to handle anger positively. Our responses to anger in the past have always made things worse. We find it hard even to believe that anger itself is not evil. We also observe the angry behavior of children, teenagers, and adults flashed before the world each day on the television screen. It seems that children are becoming murderers at earlier ages and that more teenagers and adults are becoming perpetrators of violence.

Our increasingly violent culture is no doubt the result of multiple causes, but one of those would certainly be uncontrolled anger. That is our focus in this chapter: recognizing the negative responses and rejecting them in favor of constructive ones.

RECOGNIZING EXPLOSIVE ANGER

First, we will examine what is the more observable of the two, explosive anger. For many, this is their predictable response to anger. Explosive anger expresses itself in two modes: words and actions. Verbal abuse and physical abuse are now household words in America. What is even more painful is that most of us have either given or received one or both of these. Uncontrolled anger is at the root of all such abuse.

Margaret was a screamer. When someone stirred her anger, whether child, husband, or employer, the person heard about it! Margaret prided herself on "speaking her mind." "At least people know where they stand with me," she often said. The fact is that Margaret was an out-of-control woman. Beginning as a teenager, she had developed a pattern of verbal abuse that had continued for twenty-five years.

Margaret justified her angry tirades until the day her ten-year-old daughter left her the following note. "Dear Mom, I won't be home tonight. I can't take your screaming anymore. I don't know what will happen to me, but at least I won't have to hear all the nasty things you say to me when I don't do everything you want." She signed the note, "Ginny."

Fortunately, Margaret didn't scream when she read Ginny's note. She called her pastor in tears. First she said only, "Ginny has left; I don't know where she's gone. I'm so worried about her." Then she said the most hopeful thing she had said in years. "I drove her away. I know I drove her away. My screaming and yelling drove her away." Sobbing into the phone, she admitted for the first time that her angry verbal tirades toward Ginny were wrong. The pastor wisely guided Margaret to a Christian counselor where she began the process of admitting, understanding, and changing her negative responses to anger. Fortunately also, Ginny was located within forty-eight hours and later joined her mother in counseling. Today, Ginny is a nineteen-year-old freshman at the university and has a good relationship with her mother. Margaret says that the day she got Ginny's note was the worst and best day of her life.

On the other hand, Harvey was a man of action. Whenever anyone's behavior angered Harvey, his actions revealed his inner heat. Not only had he thrown Coke bottles and telephone receivers at family members, he had often broken pencils or thrown ballpoint pens while trying to balance the checkbook. Whenever he becomes angry with "stupid drivers," he leans on the horn and often makes an obscene sign in the direction of the delinquent driver.

Judy had seen some of these characteristics in Harvey before she married him, but he had never vented his anger toward her. But within six months after their wedding, he pushed her against the wall. She knew that his behavior was something she could not condone. She wrote him the following letter and mailed it to his office. "Dear Harvey, Last night you did something I never thought you would do. In anger, you pushed me against the wall. I had seen you express anger while we were dating, but I never thought you would express it toward me. Now I know that I was wrong. I love you very much, and

I don't believe that you really want to hurt me. But I cannot take that chance. I am writing you because I want you to know that if you ever touch me again in an angry way, I will leave and stay gone until I am assured by a counselor that it is safe to live with you. I love you. Judy."

The evening after Harvey received the letter, he apologized to Judy and assured her that it would never happen again. Six months later, however, in a fit of anger, he grabbed her by the shoulders and shook her. Judy didn't say a word but the next day when he came home, Harvey found the following note: "I love you too much to stay and let you hurt me and destroy your self-esteem. I know you cannot be happy about what happened last night. I will not return until your counselor assures me that you have learned to handle your anger in a more responsible manner. Love, Judy."

Judy's quick, kind, and decisive behavior was what motivated Harvey to first call his pastor and then a counselor. He knew that he was in danger of losing Judy. He knew also that he had to learn to control his anger. After three months of individual counseling and three months of marital counseling, Judy and Harvey were reunited. That was ten years ago. There has never been another episode of physical abuse from Harvey.

ABUSIVE PATTERNS, AGGRESSIVE BEHAVIOR

Both Margaret and Harvey have developed abusive patterns in expressing their anger. Such patterns form over a period of years and typically do not change unless someone important to the individual pressures the person to get help. It is the threat of losing a significant relationship that often motivates the abuser to get help. Help is readily available, and destructive, abusive patterns can be changed. But such patterns will not simply go away with time. Family members and friends must learn to hold the explosive person accountable for his/her destructive response to anger.

Explosive, angry behavior is never constructive. It not only hurts the person at whom it is directed, it destroys the self-esteem of the person who is out of control. No one can feel good about themselves when they think about what they have done. In the heat of such angry explosions, people say and do things they later regret. Undisciplined anger that expresses itself in verbal and physical explosions will ultimately destroy relationships. The person who receives such angry explosions loses respect for the person who is out of control and will eventually lose any desire to be in his/her presence.

Some years ago it was popular in certain psychological circles to believe that releasing anger by aggressive behavior could be a positive way of processing anger if the aggression was not toward a person. Thus, angry people were encouraged to beat pillows, punching bags, and dolls or to take their aggression out on a golf ball. However, almost all research now indicates that the venting of angry feelings with such aggressive behaviors does not drain a person's anger but actually makes the person more likely to be explosive in the future.[1] Explosion, whether verbal or physical, is not an acceptable way of handling one's anger.

RECOGNIZING IMPLOSIVE ANGER

Merriam-Webster's New Collegiate Dictionary (sixth edition) defines the word *implosion* as "a bursting inwards; contrasted with explosion." The Chicago public housing building leveled by explosives was destroyed by means of implosion. In destroying any building through implosion, the wrecking crew place the destructive power within the building rather than outside, keeping all the rubble and glass inside. This is a graphic picture of what happens to the person who chooses to hold anger inside. One's life literally crumbles around internalized anger. Whereas explosive anger is readily observed by the person's screaming, swearing, condemning, criticizing, and other words or acts of rage, implosive anger is not readily recognized by others because it is, by definition, held inside.

Some Christians who would deplore explosive expressions of anger fail to reckon with the reality that implosive anger is fully as destructive in the long run. Whereas explosive anger begins with rage and may quickly turn to violence, implosive anger begins with silence and withdrawal but in time leads to resentment, bitterness, and eventually hatred. Implosive anger is typically characterized by three elements: denial, withdrawal, and brooding. Let's look at each of these.

Those who practice an implosive method of responding to anger often begin by denying that they are angry at all. This response to anger is especially tempting to Christians who have been taught that anger itself is sinful. Thus, one often hears individuals say one of the following:

• "I'm not angry, but I am very frustrated."
• "I'm not angry; I'm just upset."

79

• "I'm not angry, but I am disappointed."

• "I'm not angry; I just don't like it when people do me wrong."

In almost all these cases, however, their condition is the same: The people are experiencing anger.

Beverly illustrates this clearly. Sitting in my office on a beautiful October morning, she said to me, "Dr. Chapman, I know that Christians are not supposed to get angry and I don't think I am, but I'm so upset at what has happened that I don't know what to do. My brother talked my parents into selling their house and giving him the money to start a business. He moved them into a small apartment, promised to pay their monthly rent as long as they lived, and said that if they ever needed to go to a retirement center, by then he would be able to afford it. He did all of this without discussing the matter with me. I know my brother. His business ideas are always wild. Within two years, he will lose all the money and my parents will be on welfare.

"When I found out what had happened, I called him and he matter-of-factly told me about the whole process. He said he knew that I would not be upset because we both had talked earlier that they needed to be in a smaller place. I told him that I understood and I was sure it would work out. But the more I think about it, the more upset I get."

Beverly is obviously experiencing intense anger. Because she believes anger to be "unchristian," she doesn't want to call it anger, so she uses the word *upset*. The real denial, however, was in her conversation with her brother. She gave him the impression that his actions were acceptable, whereas in reality she found them to be unacceptable. He doesn't know that she is angry; but, in fact, she is seething inside with anger. If she doesn't change her approach, the bombs of implosion will become deeply rooted inside of her and in due time, her life will collapse. (See the likely results of implosive anger in next section.)

Denying anger does not eliminate its destructive power. Internalized anger, whether admitted or not, will have its destructive effect upon the body and psyche of the angry individual. The anger does not die with denial. Rather, it continues to expand until denial is no longer possible.

While denial is often but not always a characteristic of implosive anger, withdrawal is the central strategy of the person who practices implosive anger. While admitting anger to themselves and others, they withdraw from the person or situation that stimulated the anger. The idea is not denial but distance. *If I can stay away from the person or at least not talk to him when I am with him, perhaps my anger will diminish with time,* the angry individual reassures himself. If the offending person notices the silent withdrawal and asks, "Is something wrong?" the withdrawer will respond, "No. What makes you think something's wrong?" If the person pursues by asking, "Well, you've been quieter than usual. You haven't asked me about my day and you haven't said anything about yours," the withdrawer may respond, "I'm just tired. I had a hard day," as he walks out of the room.

RESULTS OF IMPLOSIVE ANGER

The silent, withdrawing approach to anger may last for a day or for years, but the longer this approach is taken, the more certain is resentment and bitterness.

Often this internalized anger will express itself in what the psychologists call *passive-aggressive behavior.* The person is passive on the outside, trying to give the appearance that nothing is bothering him, but eventually the anger is expressed in other ways, such as failure to comply with the request the other person makes.

Howard, for example, was expressing passive-aggressive behavior toward his wife Helen. He was angry with Helen because she expressed no interest in sexual intimacy. Though Howard refused to discuss the matter openly with Helen, when she asked him to help with the dishes, he simply continued watching television, not even acknowledging her request. When she asked him to please mow the grass on Saturday, he planned a canoe trip with his son. Most of the time Howard was not even fully conscious of what he was doing in his anger, but he was still getting back at her.

And what about Helen? Her lack of interest in sexual intimacy also could have been a passive-aggressive act. She might have been storing her own anger toward Howard because he had failed to spend quality time with her. She would not discuss the issue that stimulated her anger, but her anger had gone underground and was being expressed in her behavior. Thus, the passive-aggressive pattern becomes a vicious cycle, stimulating additional anger and additional passive-aggressive behavior. Unless this destructive cycle is broken, it is only a matter of time until their marriage implodes.

Another common result of internal anger is to redirect the buried anger.

The individual redirects his or her angry feelings away from the person or situation that stimulated the anger and toward another person or object. We are all familiar with the man who is angry with his supervisor but fears confronting the supervisor and chooses rather to come home, kick the cat, curse the children, and be verbally rude to his wife. This misplaced anger simply stimulates more anger in the people who are abused and does nothing to deal with the situation that stimulated the original anger. The people who are the recipients of this misplaced anger are left in confusion. The person who is dishing out the misplaced anger may not be conscious of the connection between his supervisor's mistreatment and what he is doing to family members. Such expressions of misplaced anger do not process the original anger. It is still buried inside the person, waiting to be processed in a more positive manner.

This suppression of anger, holding anger inside, will eventually lead to physiological and psychological stress. There is a growing body of research that shows a positive correlation between suppressed anger and hypertension, colitis, migraine headaches, and heart disease.[2] However, the more pronounced results of suppressing anger are found in its impact upon one's psychological or emotional health. Internalized anger eventually leads to resentment, bitterness, and often hatred. All of these are explicitly condemned in Scripture and are viewed as sinful responses to anger.

A third characteristic of implosive anger is brooding over the events that stimulated the anger. In the person's mind, the initial scene of wrongdoing is played over and over like a videotape. He sees the other person's facial expression; he hears the person's words; he senses his spirit; he relives the events that stimulated the angry emotions. He replays the psychological audiotapes of his own analysis of the situation.

How could he be so ungrateful? Look at the number of years I've put into the company. He's only been here five years. He has no idea what's going on. If he knew how important I am to the company, he wouldn't treat me this way. I feel like resigning and letting him suffer. Or I feel like appealing to the board and getting him fired.

On and on the tapes play as one wallows in his or her anger. The difficulty is the tapes play only in the person's head. The anger is never processed with the person involved or with a counselor or trusted friend. The anger is developing into resentment and bitterness. If the process is not interrupted, the person will eventually experience an implosion in the form of an emotional breakdown, depression, or in some cases, suicide.

However, for a growing number of these people who are internalizing anger, the end result will be not an implosion but an explosion. In their desperate emotional state, they will do some act of violence toward the person who wronged them. This is seen over and over again on the nightly news where the employee who was fired nine months ago walks in and shoots the supervisor who fired him. The child who was abused by parents, at the age of fifteen turns on the parents and murders them. The calm and meek husband turns on his wife and destroys her life. Neighbors find these realities almost incredulous. Typically, they say to the reporter, "He seemed like such a nice man. I can't believe that he would do such a thing." What the neighbor could not observe was the internalized anger that had been fed by brooding over a long period of time.

It should be obvious that implosive anger is fully as destructive as explosive anger. That is why the Scriptures always condemn internalizing anger. The apostle Paul admonished, 'In your anger do not sin': Do not let the sun go down while you are still angry, and do not give the devil a foothold" (Ephesians 4:26–27). Clearly Paul instructed that we are to process anger quickly, not allowing it to linger inside beyond sunset. I suppose that if we get angry after dark, he would give us till midnight, but the principle is that anger is not to be held inside; in fact, to do so is to give the devil a foothold. That is, we are cooperating with Satan and setting ourselves up to sin even further. The apostle further challenged us to rid ourselves of anger. (See Ephesians 4:31; Colossians 3:8.) This is not an indication that anger itself is a sin; it is an indication that to allow anger to live inside is sinful. Solomon warned that "anger resides in the lap of fools" (Ecclesiastes 7:9). The key word is *resides;* the fool lets the anger abide in him. The implication is that those who are wise will see that anger is quickly removed. Anger was designed to be a visitor, never a resident in the human heart.

All of us experience anger for the reasons noted in earlier chapters. But holding anger inside by denying, withdrawing, and brooding is not the Christian response to anger. In fact, to do so is to violate the clear teachings of Scripture. Bitterness is the result of stored anger, and bitterness is always condemned as sinful in Scripture. (For example, see Acts 8:23; Romans 3:14; Hebrews 12:15.)

WATCH OUT FOR HATE

In the course of counseling through the years, I have heard teenagers say, "I hate my father." Almost always such a statement is tied to a series of perceived wrongs committed by the father. The teenager has internalized the hurt and anger and has developed resentment, bitterness, and now hatred toward the father. I have also heard more than one wife say, "I hate my husband," and I've heard husbands express the same about their wives. Without exception, hatred does not develop overnight. Hatred is the result of internalized anger that remains planted in the heart of the individual.

Eventually the emotions of hurt from the internalized anger are replaced. In their stead appear the emotion of bitterness and the attitude of hatred. Almost always those who hate wish ill upon the person at whom they are angry. Sometimes, they end up perpetrating this ill themselves. The internalized anger erupts for all the world to observe.

When someone perpetrates evil upon the individual who wronged them, they have taken the prerogative of God. The Scriptures say, "Vengeance is mine; I will repay, saith the Lord" (Romans 12:19 KJV). When we seek to impose judgment upon those who have wronged us, we will inevitably make things worse.

What positive steps can one take to defuse implosive anger? First, admit the tendency to yourself: "It's true, I hold my anger inside. I find it very difficult to share with others that I am feeling angry. I know I am hurting myself by doing this." These are the statements that lead to help. Second, reveal your problem to a trusted friend or family member. Telling someone else and asking for their advice may help you decide whether you should confront the person or persons with whom you are angry. Perhaps you will choose to "let the offense go," but at least this will be a conscious choice, and you can release your anger. If the person to whom you disclose your anger is unable to give you the help you need, then look for a pastor or counselor who can. Don't continue the destructive response to anger.

Perhaps you know a friend who seems to be harboring anger inside. Why not take the risk of helping him or her. "I could be wrong, but I genuinely care about you, and that is why I am asking this question," you might begin. "Could it be that you are angry with someone and are holding it all inside? If I'm wrong, just tell me. But if it's true, I would like to help you process it. I know it isn't good to hold anger inside. Would you like to talk about it?"

Yes, you are running a risk by asking such questions. The person may tell you it is none of your business. On the other hand, your friend may open up, and your probing will be the first step in bringing his problem to the surface. If you are not able to help him further, then point the person to someone who can. A true friend does not sit silently and watch the self-destruction of a neighbor.

The clear challenge of Scripture is that we learn to process anger in a positive, loving manner rather than by explosion or implosion. The practice of explosive anger and implosive anger are not only highly destructive to the individual who is so handling anger but to everyone involved, including the community at large. Neither of these responses to anger can be accepted as appropriate in the life of a Christian. If you recognize either of these patterns in your own response to anger, I urge you to talk with a pastor, a counselor, or a friend; share with someone your struggle with these destructive patterns. You cannot reach your potential for God and good in the world if you continue to respond to your anger either by explosion or implosion. That brings us to the next issue in handling our anger: What about the person who has been wronged for a lifetime and has stored the anger inside and has become an angry, resentful person? In the next chapter we address that question.

NOTES

1. Mark P. Cosgrove, *Counseling for Anger* (Dallas: Word, 1988), 71, 95.
2. Ibid., 98.

CAREFUL, DO NOT IMPLODE!

*T*hough explosive responses to anger are more dramatic (and therefore more noticeable), implosive responses are more common. Contrary to what many believe, implosive reactions can be as destructive as explosive reactions. Here's a summary of the impact of implosive anger.

Nature of Implosive Anger Internalized anger that is never expressed

Motivation Fear of confrontation; belief that feeling or expressing anger is wrong

Symptoms Denial that one is angry; withdrawal from the other person

Common Statements "I'm not angry, but I am very frustrated."
"I'm not angry, but I am disappointed."

Results Passive-aggressive behavior; redirected anger toward someone else; physiological and psychological stress; can lead to resentment, bitterness, and hatred, or even to explosion in the form of a violent action.

FOR DISCUSSION

1. What are some typical attributes of explosive anger? Share a personal episode from your past where you exhibited explosive anger. Did you realize what you were doing? Did you try to control your explosive anger? How? Did prayer factor into the resolution of your anger? Discuss with the group ways to restrain explosive anger.

2. Implosive anger appears to be the opposite of explosive anger, yet it shares some core elements with explosive anger. What are the characteristics of implosive anger? Do you agree with the author that implosive is as serious as explosive anger?

3. We see few episodes of Christ's anger in the Scriptures. A notable case is His encounter with the money changers at the temple (Matthew 21:12–13). How does Christ's reaction differ from explosive anger?

4. *Processing your anger:* You are a supervisor in a large warehouse. Two of your younger employees, Frank and Juan, are frequently arguing with others in the warehouse, slowing down the processing of new inventory as well as the release of orders for customers. The arguments are usually over pay and benefits the more senior employees enjoy, but which Frank and Juan aren't yet entitled to by virtue of time on the job. When you talked to them once before, they both yelled at you in the presence of other workers. Their disturbances have seriously affected morale and productivity, but you are reluctant to fire them as they are related to senior executives in the company. Your own boss has told you "fix" the problem, citing reduced department effectiveness and hinting at an adverse performance evaluation for you. How do you handle this situation? How will you process your anger? How will you control their explosive anger?

Chapter 7

PROCESSING
LONG-TERM
ANGER

$\mathcal{M}$ike was a handsome, mild-mannered, extremely successful physician. Yet his wife, Julie, had a major complaint. For the last year, he had been snapping at her and the children for "every little thing," she said.

"I'm tired of it," she told me. "I don't know what is going on inside of him, but I know that it's not good for me and the children to continue to hear his complaints. Nothing we do pleases him."

She explained that the early years of their marriage were great; Mike was very loving and caring. He seldom ever made a critical remark. But about two years ago he began to change, and Judy reported, "It's gotten worse over the last year." I asked what might have happened two years ago to stimulate a change in Mike's behavior.

"Nothing I can think of," Julie replied. "His mother did die about that time, but she had been in a nursing home for four years and for the last year hardly knew who Mike was, so I don't think her death would have anything to do with this."

"HE SEEMS TO HAVE LOST THE SPARK"

"Is there anything else about your relationship that bothers you?" I asked. "Mike seems to have lost his enthusiasm for life," she said. "He used to be so excited about his work and the family. He was always planning things for us to do. He seldom does that anymore. He seems to have lost the spark that used to be there."

At the conclusion of our session, I learned that Mike knew and approved of his wife's visit to a counselor and was even willing to join her. But Julie had wanted to come alone. "I didn't want to be inhibited by his presence, and I didn't want to say all these things in his presence because they seem to make him look bad." I recommended that Mike come alone for the next session and after that I'd like to see both of them together. Julie agreed.

Two weeks later when Mike and I got together, I briefly described Julie's visit and my desire to see him privately to get his perception of what was going on. "Then, if both of you are willing, I'd like to see the two of you together."

"Fine," Mike said, "I know that we've got some problems, and we need to deal with them."

"As you look at the earlier years of your marriage to Julie, how would you characterize those years?" I inquired.

"We had a good marriage. We did lots of things together. We enjoyed being with each other; we had lots of fun. When the children came, even though they required a lot of time, we still made time for each other. I think we had a good marriage. In fact, I think we still have a good marriage, but things have been a little rocky for the last year or so."

MIKE'S STORY

"From your perspective, what has made the marriage rocky over the last year or so?" I inquired. "Well, I think I've been under a lot of stress at work," Mike said, "and I think the children have become more demanding for Julie. She seems to stay tired all the time. I guess we're both under a lot of stress."

"What effect has your stress had upon your behavior in the marriage?"

"Julie says I have been more critical of her and the children."

"Do you think this is true?"

"I think so. I know I verbalize my feelings a lot more, and I guess maybe I do come across as critical. I seem to get irritated easier."

"How has Julie's stress been expressed in her behavior?"

"She seems to be more sensitive, I think. She seems to get hurt more easily. She seems to have lost interest in our sexual relationship. It just doesn't seem to be important to her anymore."

"Have some of your complaints to Julie centered around the sexual part of your marriage?" I asked.

"I don't think so. At least, not often." Shaking his head, Mike said, "I don't know. Lately, I haven't had much interest myself. In fact, I seem to have lost my bounce. I'm not very excited about my work or anything else. Frankly, this bothers me more than anything."

"How long have you been feeling this way?" I inquired.

"A year or so, I guess. It just seems to have gotten worse within the last two months."

"Do you mind if I ask you some questions about your childhood?" Mike agreed, and he told me he had a younger brother and a stepsister.

"My dad left my mom when I was young," Mike continued. "He remarried and had a daughter in that marriage. She's ten years younger than I, but actually I'm closer to her than I am my brother." His brother and he "did not get along very well," Mike explained. Then he added, "With Dad being gone, we both wanted to be the man of the house. It seems like we were always fighting about something. After I went to college and he went into the military, we didn't keep in touch very much."

His father was an alcoholic, he revealed. "When he was still at home, he was OK when he wasn't drunk, but when he got drunk, he was violent. I don't have good memories of my childhood. After Dad left, we didn't see him for about five years. But when I started college, he said he wanted to help me, which he did. After that, we saw each other once in awhile, but we've never had a really close relationship."

"And what about your relationship with your mother?"

"Mom had her own problems," he said. "Maybe that's what drove Dad to drink; I don't know. She was very critical, not a warm person. After Dad left, she worked hard to make sure we had food and a place to live. I respect her for that, but she was hard on me and my brother. I was actually glad when it came time to go to college."

Unlike his father, Mike's mother did not remarry. She died about two years earlier, Mike said. In her later years she had developed Alzheimer's, and during the final three years before she died, her health steadily declined. "In the end, often she would not know who I was when I went to see her," Mike said.

"Do you think you have had a lot of resentment toward your mother and father over the years?" I asked.

"I don't know if it's resentment," he said. "I think I felt sorry for them through the years. Both of them had a rather empty life."

"Was college a good experience for you?" I asked.

"Yes and no. Well, yes, really. It was a good experience but it was also a hard experience. I did well academically, but in my social life I did some things I later regretted. They caused me a lot of trouble. To be honest with you, in my junior year, I got a girl pregnant. I wanted her to have an abortion; she wouldn't. She ended up putting the baby up for adoption, but it was a real hassle. Julie knows about this, but we have never told the kids. I don't think they need to know."

I could tell that Mike was being very vulnerable with me. I could also tell that he was beginning to feel uncomfortable. "When you're driving a car and you're stopped at a traffic light, when the light turns green and the person in front of you doesn't move immediately, do you blow the horn?" Michael smiled, was silent for a moment, and then said, "How did you know?"

"I'm only asking," I said.

"I'm guilty," he replied. "I'm usually a calm man at my work and at home. And in all my relationships, I'm known as 'the steady one.' But when I get behind the wheel, I guess all my hostility comes out. You know, people do stupid things, so I yell at them if I'm by myself. If Julie and the kids are in the car, I try to keep it under control."

"Have you always been a horn blower?" I asked.

"I think so," he said smiling. "I remember doing that in high school. Yeah, I guess I've always been a horn blower." Now Mike is laughing aloud at himself and I'm laughing with him.

"I want to give you some food for thought," I continued. "My guess is that you are a very angry man, that you have stored inside lots of anger over a long period of time."

Mike was silent for a moment, then said, "I never thought of myself as an angry person. In fact, I've always prided myself on handling my anger. I'm not the explosive type. I learned early on that it doesn't pay to fight. I don't see myself as an angry person," he concluded. I nodded and said, "You may be right. We'll explore that further next time."

MIKE'S ASSIGNMENT

"I want to give you an assignment this week that will take a little time, at least an hour or an hour and one-half. I want to ask that you get alone with pencil and paper. And I want you to think through your life, answering two questions: *Who are the people who have wronged me? and What have they done?* You may want to make two columns on your paper, one entitled 'People' and the other 'Ways they have wronged me.' Begin with your earliest memory; focus on your childhood, your relationships with your mother, father, and brother. If all of them wronged you at one time or another, which would be pretty normal, list their names and list the ways in which they wronged you. Be specific when you have specific memories. For example, if your brother hit you over the head with a ball bat, put it down: 'Ned hit me with a ball bat when I was ten.' Be as specific and detailed as you can.

"Once you have finished with your family, take a look at your school career; go back as early as you can remember. Did a teacher or student wrong you? If so, put the person's name and what he or she did. Then look at other relationships that you may have had during childhood, relationships at church, in the neighborhood, during the teenage years, dating relationships. List everything that comes to mind. Then move to the college years. Think in terms of professors, fellow students, girlfriends, or others. Then go through your medical school experience, your residency, and all of your vocational settings up until the present. Then look at your relationship with Julie and the children. Begin with your dating relationship and move through your marriage.

"Think about your relationships with your extended family, business associates, and others. Try to be as comprehensive as you can. You can see why I said that this may take some time. I think it will be very helpful, so I want to ask you to give it your best efforts." I sensed that Mike didn't know exactly where we were going with all of this, but he was intrigued with the idea and readily agreed. "I would also like to suggest that the two of us meet one more time before we invite Julie to join us." "Fine," he said. "I'll tell Julie."

Two weeks later, Mike returned to my office with a yellow legal pad with three pages of names and events where he had been wronged throughout his life. "This assignment was very revealing," he said. "I've never thought about this before and I never anticipated that I would come up with all of this. But once I started, my memory kicked in and it flowed faster than I could write.

Actually, it was a very painful experience. I've never spent this much time thinking about my past. I've always been busy accomplishing my goals. My philosophy has been 'You can't change the past, so why bother with it?'"

"There's some truth to that philosophy," I replied, "but there are two other realities. One is that we can learn from the past and the other is that the past often affects our present behavior."

I took Mike's list, read his father's name first, and silently read the statements describing the wrongs that his father had done. Then I looked at Mike and asked, "Did you ever share these things with your father?"

"No," he said. "I learned early that you don't talk with my father, especially if you disagree with him."

I nodded my head, silently looked back at the legal pad in front of me, and read the things he had beside his mother's name. Then I asked, "Did you ever share any of these things with your mother?" "No, I didn't want to hurt Mom. She'd been through enough. I just tried to keep peace with her." I glanced down, reading his brother's name and the list beside his name. "Did you share any of these with your brother?" I asked.

"Well, when we were both at home, yes. Actually we fought about most of those things."

I continued down the list one by one, reading the names and events of people who had wronged Mike through the years. There were thirty-four names and numerous events. In only two cases had Mike processed his anger in a positive way. In the other thirty-two cases, Mike had simply "tried to forget it" and focus on the future.

DEALING WITH STORED ANGER

"Do you understand now why I guessed in our last session that you had a lot of anger stored inside?"

"I think you were right," Mike said, "but how did you know?"

"Because you exhibited two common traits of stored anger," I continued. "One is to use your words—you 'complained a lot' about Julie and the children's behavior. To use Julie's words, you 'snapped at [her]' and the children. The other is your lethargic behavior over the past several months. To use your words, you've 'lost your bounce.' To use Julie's words, you 'seem to have lost the spark that used to be there.' I want to share with you why I believe this has happened.

"Throughout your lifetime, you have suffered some rather severe injustices. Understand, I'm not suggesting that all the people who have wronged you are bad people. What I'm observing is that a number of people in your life have done things that have deeply hurt you. Whenever we are wronged, anger is the natural emotion which arises within. The healthy way of handling that anger is to lovingly confront the person who has wronged us and work through it, seeking a resolution. Often, however, because of various circumstances, we are not able to do that. Children, for example, seldom process their anger toward parents—normally out of fear that the parents will not understand or will make things even worse. Thus, your response of not confronting your parents with your anger is very normal for children and teenagers.

"With your younger brother, you did process your anger somewhat by verbally arguing with each other and sometimes physically fighting each other. Neither of these led to a resolution of the issues which stimulated the anger. In most of the other situations that you have described, your response was to try to forget about the wrong which had been inflicted and to go on with your life. However, anger is not resolved that easily. In fact, wrongs are not forgotten unless they are processed. The fact that you can remember these several years after they happened indicates that you have not really forgotten them."

Mike was listening quietly, nodding his head at key points. I continued.

"Whenever we have experienced a series of wrongs over a long period of time, our emotional ability to absorb these wrongs is stretched beyond capacity. One of two things begins to happen. We begin to express this anger not toward the people who perpetrated it through the years but toward other people in our present setting—in your case, toward Julie and the children. So you began to verbalize your anger by making critical remarks toward them. That is clearly a different approach from the one you have made through the years. The second way your anger is evidenced is by the beginning stages of depression.

"The purpose of our anger is to motivate us to take constructive action with the person who has wronged us, but if we fail to do this, unresolved anger becomes a dark cloud over our lives. We have been wronged, wronged, wronged—wronged throughout our lives by numerous people in numerous ways. The heaviness of all that injustice begins to settle upon our emotions.

95

And we find ourselves becoming lethargic toward life, no longer interested in the things that used to stimulate our interest. If positive steps are not taken, the person goes on to become more and more explosive and/or more and more depressed."

Mike had been nodding his head for the last five minutes. "It all makes a lot of sense," he said. "But why did all of this just start happening only recently?"

"I think it was triggered by your mother's death," I responded. "Even though she had been sick and in the nursing home for the last three years of her life, I think her death touched the deep unresolved emotions that were inside and brought all this to the surface again. Before that time, the unresolved anger was covered by layers of activity that kept the conscious mind occupied on reaching worthwhile goals."

"Like a latent infection," Mike interjected, "waiting for a stimulant."

"Exactly," I responded.

"That makes a lot of sense," Mike said. "But what am I gonna do about it? I can't go back and talk to all these people. My mother's dead; my father would never understand. Some of the other people are also dead, and others, I have no idea where they live."

Now I am the one nodding in agreement. "That's true," I said, "so I'm going to make another suggestion. What I'm going to suggest will not rebuild relationships with any of these people. In fact, some of the people you no longer have a relationship with anyway. But what I'm going to suggest will process your anger in a positive way and allow you to change the two negative behaviors you are now experiencing."

I knew that Mike was a strong Christian and that he would understand the biblical foundation for what I was about to suggest. "I want to begin by reminding you about two basic fundamental characteristics of God. God is loving and God is just. God cares about the well-being of His creatures, but God is also just and ultimately will bring all men to justice. As Christians, we understand this. That's what the Cross is all about—Christ took the full penalty of our sins. And those who will accept that God can forgive and still be just.[1]

There's one other biblical concept that I want to remind you of. The Scriptures say that "Vengeance is mine; I will repay, saith the Lord.'"[2] It is never our job to vindicate ourselves by making people pay for the wrongs they've done toward us. They will either confess those wrongs to God and experience His forgiveness based upon what Christ has done for them, or they will face God with those sins and He will be the ultimate and final judge."

ALONE WITH GOD

"Now here is what I want to suggest," I said, looking directly at Mike. "As soon as possible, I want you to take this legal pad and get alone with God. I want you to read each name and each offense to God; read it aloud. Then say to God, 'You know what my father did—this and this and this and this. And You know how wrong it was for a father to do these things to a child, and You know how much they hurt me. They've been inside all these years. But today, I want to release my father and all of these wrongs to You. You are a just God, and You are a loving God. You know everything about my father. I don't know what motivated him to do these things. You know his motives as well as his actions. And so I want to put him into Your hands and let You take care of him.

"'Do whatever You wish, whatever is good, whatever is loving. I put him into Your hands and I release all of these wrongs to You, knowing that if he confesses them, You will forgive him. If not, You will deal with him on these matters. But I release them and give them to You today.'

"I want you to go through your whole list, everyone's name and everyone's actions and release them to God one by one, wrong by wrong," I told Mike. "Release them to God. Once you've done that, I want you to thank God that all of these things are now released to Him. And I want you to ask God to fill your life with His Holy Spirit and give you the power to be the man He wants you to be in the future. And also ask Him for the ability to process future anger experiences when they occur. People will continue to do you wrong. Even Julie will do you wrong, and your children may do you wrong. But we are going to talk about how to process that anger in a positive way, and that's what I want you to learn.

"So you are going to ask God to teach you how to process your anger. Then as a symbol that you have released all these things to God and they are no longer in your life but in His hands, I want you either to burn or tear up and destroy these lists."

Two weeks later, Mike and Julie returned. Both were smiling. Mike had shared with her what he had done. "It's been a good two weeks," Julie said. "This is one of the greatest things that has ever happened in our lives. I feel like I've got a new husband."

"It's been a good two weeks," Mike said. "The process of sharing those things with Julie was hard; sharing them with God was easier. But I feel like a load has been lifted."

"He hasn't been critical a single time this week," Julie said.

"Well, the anger is gone," Mike replied. "There's no need to be critical, and I'm beginning to feel excited about life again."

The rest of the session was spent helping Mike and Julie establish new guidelines for handling their anger in the future. Those guidelines are found in chapter 3. We had two more sessions dealing with other minor issues in their relationship. Mike and Julie had passed a significant milestone in their marriage, one that has greatly enhanced their marital intimacy and has enabled them to help many other couples over the past ten years.

WHEN ANGER CONTINUES
FOR THE LONG TERM

After twenty-five years of counseling, I am convinced there are thousands of Mikes in the world, many of them extremely successful in their vocation and for many years untroubled by their hidden anger. But sooner or later, unprocessed anger will express itself either in violent behavior normally toward innocent people or in deep, unresolved depression, which keeps the individual from reaching his/her potential for God and good in the world. Please do not hear me saying that all depression is caused by unresolved anger. This is certainly not the case. But depression is sometimes the result of anger which is stored inside the individual over a long period of time.

When anger remains for the long term, we must process it to avoid those explosive or implosive responses. The process I have described in this chapter by sharing Mike's story would be helpful for anyone. Many people like Mike are totally unaware that past experiences are affecting their present behavior. Making a list of the wrongs perpetrated against us through the years is the first step in identifying unprocessed anger. Once the list is made, you may ask yourself, "How did I process my anger over this event?" If you find that it was not processed or processed poorly, then it is never too late to deal with unresolved anger.

Let me reiterate, however, what I said to Mike: Processing our anger with God in this manner does not in and of itself rebuild relationships with the

people who have wronged us. Rather it brings emotional and spiritual healing to us. Equally important, it makes our lives different in the future.

Whether one should go back and seek to deal personally with the individuals who wronged us is a decision that requires prayer and careful
thought. There are numerous factors to consider, most of which we discussed
in chapter 3 when we talked about processing anger with the person who
wronged us. Where this can be done, it brings the potential not only of personal healing but of healing the relationship. At the same time, it brings the
potential for further rejection, hurt, and wrong. If the person is still alive and
the relationship is still important, I recommend one prayerfully consider this
alternative. Usually such an attempt at reconciliation will be more productive
if the individual has the assistance of a trusted pastor, counselor, or friend.

Such reconciliation always requires forgiveness. That brings us to the
topic of chapter 8: "Anger and Forgiveness."

NOTES

1. See Romans 3:26.
2. Romans 12:19 KJV.

RECOGNIZING AND PROCESSING
YOUR LONG-TERM ANGER

*W*hen anger continues for years, the consequences can be severe, either physiologically or emotionally. But like Mike, you can process your unresolved anger. There are at least four and sometimes as many as six steps in processing long-term anger.

First, make a list of wrongs perpetuated against you through the years.

Second, look at the list and ask yourself, "How did I process my anger over this event?" This will help you identify any unprocessed anger. Remember, no matter how long ago the event occurred, it is never too late to deal with the unresolved anger.

Third, release your anger to God and thank God that He will deal justly and lovingly with those who have wronged you. Take this step for those who are no longer living or available to reconcile.

Fourth, for those still living, decide whether to seek reconciliation or to "let the offense go." If you choose to overlook the offense, then express this decision to God. In prayer, confess your anger and your willingness to turn the person over to the righteous and just God. Then release your anger to Him. (See chapter 3 for more information on letting go.)

If you decide to proceed with reconciliation, I recommend a *fifth step: Bring a compassionate third party to the meeting.* Take a trusted pastor, counselor, or friend to your meeting. The third party can act as a mediator or facilitator during the dispute, can recognize when the dialogue is moving off track and return the two to the main issue, and, as a witness, will remind both parties of the importance and urgency of such reconciliation.

With reconciliation, move also to a *sixth step: Seek forgiveness.* Reconciliation almost always requires forgiveness, usually by you, but sometimes by the other party, whom you have perhaps unintentionally offended. (We will discuss the approach to forgiveness in chapter 8.)

FOR DISCUSSION

1. Most people have experienced or are experiencing some long-term anger that has not been adequately resolved. Usually the subject is too painful or difficult to raise with the other person. Identify some instance of long-term anger that you have wrestled with. What was the nature of the problem? At whom was the anger directed? Why couldn't the anger be resolved earlier? If resolved, how was this accomplished? Share experiences in the group and record common cords between stories.

2. Parents often play a large role in developing and/or resolving long-term anger. As a parent, how can you make it easier to resolve long-term anger and frustrations with your children? As an adult child, how can you make it easier to resolve long-term anger with your parents? What conditions must be present for resolution to occur? What conditions stifle parent-child anger resolution?

3. Long-term anger may be present but not recognizable in ourselves. What can you do to recognize the signs of long-term anger? How can you resolve it?

4. *Processing your anger:* Your father is a retired high school basketball coach. Despite your great enthusiasm for sports and basketball in particular, your father never devoted the time to develop you as a player, instead concentrating on your friends who "had what it takes." Many of them went on to play in college, and one even became a professional basketball player. You made your father's team, but spent most of your time warming the bench. Now that your own son is interested in sports, you are determined not to be the "failure" your father was to his children. You are angry with your father and become reluctant to expose him to his grandchildren. How will you resolve this anger?

101

Chapter 8

ANGER AND FORGIVENESS

*M*arilyn has just learned that her husband of ten years is having an affair with a young woman in his office. Marilyn is hurt and angry.

Phil has spent months working on an innovative idea, which he thinks will save his company thousands of dollars per year. Last month, he shared his idea with a colleague. Two weeks later, his colleague submitted to the administration a slightly modified version of Phil's idea with no mention of Phil. Phil found out about it two weeks later when his supervisor shared the idea with him to get his feedback. Phil is enraged.

Rachel, a high school sophomore, had worked all summer getting ready for the cheerleader tryouts. When the tryouts were over, she felt good about her performance. A week later she discovered that she was not selected. She was crushed. Four days later she found out that Lisa, whom she thought to be her friend, had lied to the cheerleading coach, telling her that Rachel was using drugs. Rachel is livid with anger.

Different people, different situations. Yet Marilyn, Phil, and Rachel all demonstrate a common principle at work. Valid anger is always stimulated by injustice. Marilyn was sinned against by her husband. Phil's colleague treated him unfairly. Rachel's friend Lisa treated her unjustly. All three have valid anger—responses to actual injustices.

As we discussed in chapter 1, we have the capacity for anger because we are moral creatures. Even in the worst of us, there is some concern for rightness. Anger is our emotional, spiritual, and physical response when we encounter injustice. The Bible calls this injustice sin.

SEPARATION . . . AND FORGIVENESS BY GOD

When one person sins against another, it always creates distance between the two of them. This reality is evidenced throughout Scripture, beginning with Adam and Eve, who before their sin enjoyed fellowship with God in the Garden. But after their sin, they found themselves not only hiding from God but estranged from each other. Adam was blaming Eve; Eve was blaming the serpent. That's not exactly a picture of domestic tranquillity.

Later the prophet Isaiah thundered this message to ancient Israel: "Your iniquities have separated you from your God; your sins have hidden his face from you, so that he will not hear" (Isaiah 59:2). We are never separated from God's love, but sin does separate us from His fellowship. The New Testament reminds us that "the wages of sin is death." Death is the ultimate picture of separation. Of course, this is not what God desires for His creatures; therefore, the writer quickly adds, "The gift of God is eternal life in Christ Jesus our Lord" (Romans 6:23). God desires fellowship with His creatures. That is what the cross of Christ is all about. God offers His forgiveness and the gift of eternal life.

In order to experience God's forgiveness, man must respond to the call of God's spirit by repentance and faith in Christ. (See Acts 2:37–39.)

The word *repent* means literally "to turn around." The message is clear: If we would receive God's forgiveness and enter into His eternal family, we must turn from our sin, acknowledge that Christ has paid the ultimate penalty for our sins, and accept God's forgiveness and gift of eternal life—all of this at the urging and guiding of the Holy Spirit.

The Scripture describes this new believer in Christ as "a newborn baby" who must grow up into Christlikeness. God's objective is clear: He wants His children to become like Christ. (See 1 Peter 2:2–5, 9–12; Romans 8:29.) However, this does not happen instantly. It is a process, and because our sinful nature is not eradicated, there is always the possibility that we will momentarily turn from God's purposes and fail to follow the teachings of Jesus. Again the biblical word for this failure is *sin*.

A loving God will forgive all who acknowledge their sins. "If we confess our sins," the apostle John wrote, "[God] is faithful and just and will forgive us our sins and purify us from all unrighteousness" (1 John 1:9). Thus, in order for our fellowship with God to be restored, we must acknowledge our sin, thank God that Christ has paid our penalty, and reach out to accept God's forgiveness. The moment we do this, we experience the warm embrace of our heavenly Father. The distance is gone. To use John's words, we are now walking in the light, having fellowship with God. "And the blood of Jesus, his Son, purifies us from all sin" (1 John 1:7).

Before we go further, let's clarify the meaning of the word *forgiveness*. Three Hebrew words and four Greek words are translated *forgive* in the English Scriptures. They are basically synonyms with slightly varying shades of meaning. The key ideas are to cover, to take away, to pardon, and to be gracious to. The most common of these is the idea of taking away one's sins. For example, the psalmist says, "As far as the east is from the west, so far has he removed our transgressions from us" (Psalm 103:12). Thus, God's forgiveness is relieving the person from God's judgment—from the penalty due the sinner. Again the psalmist says, "He does not treat us as our sins deserve or repay us according to our iniquities" (Psalm 103:10). Isaiah the prophet spoke of God "blotting out" our sins and remembering them no more against us (Isaiah 43:25). Clearly God's forgiveness means that our sins no longer stand as a barrier between us and God. Forgiveness removes the distance and allows us open fellowship with God.

ESSENTIALS TO FORGIVING: CONFESSION AND REPENTANCE

I have taken time in these paragraphs to review God's forgiveness toward us because the Scriptures say that we are to forgive each other, "just as in Christ God forgave you" (Ephesians 4:32). Thus God's forgiveness of us serves as the model of how we are to forgive others. In this divine model, there are two essential elements—confession and repentance on the part of the sinner and forgiveness on the part of the one sinned against. In the Scriptures, these two are never separated.

For example, God's call to Israel was "'Return, faithless Israel, . . . I will frown on you no longer, for I am merciful. . . . I will not be angry forever. Only acknowledge your guilt—you have rebelled against the Lord your God, you have scattered your favors to foreign gods. . . . Return, faithless people,' declares the Lord, 'for I am your husband'" (Jeremiah 3:12–14). Never does God agree to reconcile while Israel continues in sin. There can be no reconciliation without repentance. In the New Testament, Jesus expressed the same reality when He said, "O Jerusalem, Jerusalem, you who kill the prophets and stone those sent to you, how often I longed to gather your children together, as a hen gathers her chicks under her wings, but you were not willing. Look, your house is left to you desolate" (Matthew 23:37–38). God cannot be reconciled to those who are unwilling to turn to Him.

There is no scriptural evidence that God ever forgave anyone who did not repent of sin and turn in faith to Him. Some would object by raising the following question: What about Jesus' prayer on the cross, "Father, forgive them, for they do not know what they are doing" (Luke 23:34)? Was that prayer not answered by the Father? My response is "Yes, but not immediately." Not only were they not immediately forgiven, but they continued in the dastardly act of crucifying the Son of God.

That they were not forgiven immediately is clear from Peter's sermon recorded in Acts 2, which took place on the Day of Pentecost. Peter spoke to many of those who were responsible for the crucifixion of Christ when he said, "Men of Israel, listen to this: Jesus of Nazareth was a man accredited by God to you by miracles, wonders and signs, which God did among you through him, as you yourselves know. This man . . . you, with the help of wicked men, put . . . to death by nailing him to the cross. But God raised him from the dead. . . . With many other words he warned them; and he pleaded with them" (Acts 2:22–24, 40). He was obviously preaching to some who actually participated in the crucifixion of Christ. More than three thousand responded to the truth and acknowledged Christ as Savior (verse 41). The rest of Acts records numerous others who responded to Christ. And in Acts 6:7 we read, "The number of disciples in Jerusalem increased rapidly, and a large number of priests became obedient to the faith." Apparently, it was after Pentecost when many of those who crucified Jesus came to acknowledge Him as the Messiah and experienced God's forgiveness. Jesus' prayer on the cross, "Father, forgive them, for they do not know what they are doing," is an indication of His willingness and deep desire that they experience the Father's forgiveness. It is this willingness to forgive that we must emulate. But those for whom He prayed did not experience the Father's forgiveness until they repented and placed their faith in Christ the Messiah.

SEEKING ANOTHER'S REPENTANCE

Human forgiveness is to be modeled after divine forgiveness. Confession and repentance on the part of the one sinning and forgiveness on the part of the one sinned against are still the two essential elements to genuine reconciliation. Let's go back to the three people we met at the beginning of this chapter. Marilyn's husband of ten years had been unfaithful to her and was involved in a sexual relationship with a young woman whom he had met at work. Marilyn experienced deep hurt and anger. What is she to do? Phil's colleague had betrayed him by taking his idea and submitting it as his own. Phil is furious. What is he to do? Rachel was livid with anger when she discovered that her supposed friend had lied about her use of drugs, thus thwarting Rachel's efforts to be on the cheerleading team. What is Rachel to do?

Let's look at the clear biblical paradigm laid out by Jesus in Luke 17. "If your brother sins, rebuke him, and if he repents, forgive him. If he sins against you seven times in a day, and seven times comes back to you and says 'I repent,' forgive him" (verses 3–4). Notice the progression of events. First, there is a sin committed—your brother, sister, or friend treats you unjustly. Immediately you experience valid righteous anger. Your first response is clear: You are to rebuke the person who sinned against you. As noted earlier, the word *rebuke* means to place a weight upon, to bring a matter to the attention of. In short, you confront the other person with his or her sin.

As noted earlier, it is usually best to give yourself time to cool down emotionally before you make this rebuke. But to think that you are going to be totally calm when you have been sinned against in such a radical way is to be unrealistic. However, you must be careful not to sin in your rebuke. You must treat the person as one for whom Christ died. You must exhibit Christian love in that your deepest desire is that the person will confess and repent of his wrong so that you may extend forgiveness. As Jesus was willing to forgive those who were putting Him to death, we with the help of God's Holy Spirit must be willing to forgive those who have caused us deep pain.

The next step is that the person who has sinned must repent; that is, he must confess the wrong committed and express a desire to turn from practicing that wrong in the future. If this is done, then Jesus said we are to forgive the person. We are to lift the penalty and receive the individual back into a restored relationship with us. And we begin the process of rebuilding trust. We refuse to allow someone's misdeed to keep us away from them, and we do not allow our feelings of hurt and disappointment to control our behavior toward them. We forgive them in the same manner that God has forgiven us and in the same manner that we hope they will forgive us if we sin against them.

It must be noted that forgiveness does not remove all the results of sin. When David sinned against Bathsheba and Bathsheba's husband, God fully forgave David when he confessed his sin. But the negative results of David's sin plagued him throughout the remainder of his life. The same is true of our sin. Let me illustrate. Let's say that I commit the sin of drunkenness, and in my drunken state I drive my car down the highway. A short time later, I veer off the road, run into a utility pole, and in so doing break my leg and extensively damage my car. I may confess my sin to God before I get out of the car and experience God's forgiveness. But my leg is still broken and my car is still twisted, even though I am forgiven by God. My wife shows up at the scene, and now I am faced with the reality that I have sinned against her. If I confess my wrong to her and if she chooses to forgive me, I now have the opportunity for rebuilding her trust in me. But she too will suffer; she too will be affected when our car insurance rate goes up because of my accident, and when my license is removed and she must drive me to work. I am forgiven by my wife and God, but I must continue to face the results of my wrong as the news spreads through the community. No, forgiveness does not remove all the results of sin. I must be held accountable for my actions and I must seek to learn through my failures.

A second reality of forgiveness is that forgiveness does not remove all of my painful emotions. My wife may well forgive me but when she thinks about what I did, she may once again feel disappointment and anger toward me. Forgiveness is not a feeling; it is a commitment to accept the person in spite of what they have done. It is a decision not to demand justice but to show mercy; that is what the forgiving wife (or husband) must do. Nor does forgiveness mean that I will never think of the situation again. Because every event in life is recorded in the brain, there is every potential that the event will return to the conscious mind again and again. If we have chosen to forgive, we take the memory to God along with the hurt feelings, acknowledge to Him what we are thinking and feeling, but thank Him that by His grace that has been forgiven. Then we ask Him for the power to do something kind and loving for that person today. We choose to focus on the future and not allow our minds to be obsessed with past failures that are now forgiven.

WHEN THE PERSON DOES NOT REPENT

But what if the person does not repent? Am I still to forgive the person? The biblical answer is clear, and it is found in the teachings of Jesus. "If your brother sins against you, go and show him his fault, just between the two of you. If he listens to you, you have won your brother over. But if he will not listen, take one or two others along, so that 'every matter may be established by the testimony of two or three witnesses.' If he refuses to listen to them, tell it to the church; and if he refuses to listen even to the church, treat him as you would a pagan or a tax collector" (Matthew 18:15–17). The principles of church discipline delineated by Jesus apply fully as well in any close relationship we have (including non-Christians), and it answers the question as to what we do if the person does not repent after our loving confrontation. We broaden the circle of experience by inviting two trusted friends to join us in confronting the erring person once again. If there is still no repentance, then we treat the person as a pagan, even if the individual is a believer.

How does the Christian treat pagans? We pray for them, we seek to be kind to them, but we do not treat them as though they were innocent, for they are not. Remember, all sin brings separation. The separation is not removed by our choosing to overlook the sin. Sin always creates barriers in human relationships, and the barriers only come down when there is genuine repentance and genuine forgiveness.

Let's return to Marilyn, whose husband is having an affair outside the marriage. Marilyn becomes aware of this reality. She confronts her husband with what she has discovered. He may have one of several responses. He may deny the allegations until he is convinced she has evidence. He may confess and promise her that he will sever the relationship with the young woman at work. He may tell her that he is in love with the young woman and that he wants a divorce so he can marry her. He may confess and actually break the relationship with the other person. It is only the last of these options that will make forgiveness possible. Genuine confession and genuine repentance is essential if Marilyn is to give and he is to receive genuine forgiveness. If there is genuine repentance and genuine forgiveness, then together they can work on rebuilding their marital relationship.

Let's look at Phil's situation. If Phil confronts his colleague with the wrong he has done, his colleague again has several options. He may argue that the idea which he submitted is different from Phil's original idea and that he did no wrong. He may claim that once an idea is shared, it is no longer the personal property of an individual and that Phil was foolish to share the idea with him if he didn't want it to be submitted by someone else. Or he may confess that what he did was wrong and that it has been bothering him and if Phil will forgive him, he will go to the supervisor and tell the truth. Only the last response will make genuine forgiveness possible. Until the colleague is willing to admit that he has committed a wrong, he can never experience forgiveness. Forgiveness presupposes that a wrong has been committed. If there is no wrong, there is no need for forgiveness.

SHOULD WE FORGIVE THE PERSON TO AVOID PERSONAL BITTERNESS?

Some will object by suggesting that Phil should forgive his colleague for Phil's own benefit; that he should not allow his anger to turn into bitterness toward his colleague, but rather he should forgive his colleague and release his anger. I would certainly agree to the last part of that statement—Phil should release his anger before it turns to bitterness. But the first part of the statement, from a biblical perspective, is impossible. Forgiveness, like communication, requires two parties. Forgiveness is a gift, one that cannot be opened until the sinner is willing to admit that "I need it and I want it."

There is no scriptural evidence that God ever forgives the unconfessing, unrepenting sinner. God is always willing to forgive, desirous of forgiving, but He cannot actually forgive until the sinner repents. The same is true in human relationships. Christians with the aid of the Holy Spirit must always stand ready to forgive, willing and desirous of forgiving, extending forgiveness, but we cannot force forgiveness to someone who does not desire it.

What then should Christians do with their angry feelings and thoughts when the person who wronged them refuses to repent of the wrong committed? I believe that we are to lovingly confront the person as God confronts us. If the individual does not respond positively to our first confrontation, I believe we are to pray for him and make another attempt, perhaps inviting one or two others to go with us; thus, broadening the circle of knowledge about the sin. If the person does not respond in due time to this confrontation, then the reality of the sin must be shared with the larger community, which typically involves the extended family and in some cases, the church family. If the person still does not repent of the wrong, then he or she is to be treated as a "pagan." This is the word Jesus used. The Matthew 18 passage primarily addresses relationships between Christian believers, but the principle applies to all who would let sin fracture a relationship. A pagan was an outsider, an unbeliever. Whether the offending person is an actual unbeliever or just an unrepentant sinner, we treat the individual the same, as one who has broken fellowship with us. To treat the person as a pagan means we do not regard him as a close friend. We should continue to pray for him, to be kind to him, to treat him with dignity and respect. Remember, here is a person for whom Christ died, a person with whom we would desire to be reconciled. But we cannot act as though the sin does not exist. The fact is the sin has created a barrier between the two of you, and the barrier will not dissolve with time alone.

I am often frustrated when I hear Christians admonish each other that they must forgive the offending party even if the person is unwilling to confess and repent of his sin. How many Christian wives have been put in an untenable position by pastors who encourage them to forgive husbands who are having affairs even though the husband refuses to repent. I understand the intention of the pastor's advice. He wants the wife to be free of the anger, bitterness, and perhaps hatred that has built up in her heart toward the husband and is destroying her own well-being. He desires to see her freed from all of that and walking in fellowship with God, not allowing her husband's sin to destroy her life. This intention is wholly admirable, but a nonbiblical forgiveness is not the answer.

TWO DECISIVE STEPS:
RELEASE TO GOD, CONFESS ANY PERSONAL SIN

I believe the answer lies in taking two decisive steps. *First, commit or release the person who has sinned against you to God,* letting God take care of that person rather than insisting that you pay him back for the wrongful action. The Scriptures teach that vengeance belongs to God, not to man. (See Romans 12:19.) The reason for this is that God alone knows everything about the other person, not only his actions but his motives. And God alone is judge. So the person who is eaten up with bitterness toward another who has treated him unfairly is to release that person to an all-knowing heavenly Father who is fully capable of doing what is just and right toward that person.

The apostle Paul demonstrated this when he said to young Timothy,

"Alexander the metalworker did me a great deal of harm. The Lord will repay him for what he has done. You too should be on your guard against him, because he strongly opposed our message" (2 Timothy 4:14–15). Not only had Paul not forgiven Alexander because Alexander had not repented, Paul warned Timothy to be on his guard because Alexander may also treat him unjustly. Paul did not whitewash the matter by offering an easy forgiveness to Alexander. Instead, he did the responsible thing by turning Alexander over to God. After Paul made this decision, I don't think he lost any sleep over Alexander. His anger was processed by the conscious act of turning the offender over to a just and merciful God.

Peter indicated that our Lord Himself took a similar approach. Having discussed the sufferings of Christ, Peter said, "When they hurled their insults at him, he did not retaliate; when he suffered, he made no threats. Instead, he entrusted himself to him who judges justly" (1 Peter 2:23). Or as Weymouth translates it, "He left his cause in the hands of the Righteous Judge." As a man, Jesus did not take the prerogative of taking revenge on those who had wronged Him; rather He committed the whole situation to God, knowing that God would judge righteously. Often when we have been wronged, we think that if we don't press the issue and demand justice, then no one will. The fact is God is in a far better position to be the judge than we. You can turn your erring friend and the wrong committed against you over to God, knowing that He will take the best possible action on your behalf. He is more concerned about righteousness than are you.

The *second* crucial step is for the person who has been sinned against to *confess any of his own sin*. Remember, anger itself is not sin, but often we allow anger to lead us to sinful behavior, such as an explosion or implosion (discussed in chapter 6). Thus angry employees returning to shoot it out with the supervisor are sinful; they are committing their own wrong and are compounding the problem. However, when we unleash verbal tirades against the person who has wronged us or if we commit acts of physical violence, we also are sinful. And let's not forget implosive anger: Anger held inside often becomes bitterness and hatred, both of which are condemned in Scripture as sinful.

As noted in an earlier chapter, anger was designed to be a visitor, never a resident. The biblical challenge is that we are to rid ourselves "of all such things as these: anger, rage, malice, slander, and filthy language" (Colossians

3:8). When you or I become obsessed with our own hurt and anger, we are no longer focusing on God and are guilty of misguided passion. If ever there is a time when we need the help and guidance of God, it is when we have been wronged by a friend or family member.

At that point, prayer is vital. The following prayer may help you take these two steps toward alleviating your own inner turmoil.

> Father, You know the pain, the hurt, the anger, the bitterness that I feel toward _____. You know what he (she) has done to me. You know that I have made every effort to seek reconciliation but he is unwilling to deal with the wrong. You know his response to me and You know his continued lifestyle. I recognize that he is beyond my control. I cannot make him do what I wish he would do. So I want to commit _____ to You, knowing that You are a just and honest God and that in the future, You will treat him justly. So I put _____ in Your hands and trust You to work in his life what is best.
>
> I also want to confess that I have allowed his wrong to consume me. I have become obsessed with my anger, my hurt, my disappointment, my frustration. I've had a bitter spirit toward this person, sometimes toward You for allowing this to happen. I want to confess that this is wrong, and I want to thank You that Christ has paid my penalty. I want to accept Your forgiveness for my wrong attitudes.
>
> I pray that Your Spirit will fill my heart and my mind and help me to think Your thoughts and to do only those things that will be helpful in my situation. I don't want my life to be ruined because of what the other person has done to me, and I know that is not Your desire. Guide me today as I read Your Word, as I seek the right kind of Christian friends, as I look for Christian books that will help me, as I seek to put my life back in Your hands. I want to follow You. I want to accomplish Your purposes. Let this be a day of new beginnings for me. In the name of Christ, my Savior and Lord. Amen.

Such a prayer, prayed sincerely, will channel the Christian's energies in the right direction, namely toward seeking God's fellowship and wisdom. If and when the other person confesses and repents of wrongdoing, we must stand ready to forgive and work at rebuilding the relationship.

In the meantime, we are walking in the light, having fellowship with God, knowing that God's purposes for our lives will not be thwarted because of what someone else has done. In fact, the Scriptures say that God will turn even the wrongs done to us into something positive. (See Romans 8:28–29.) Let me be clear in noting that such action does not restore the fellowship with the person who has wronged you, but it does liberate you to go on with your life and to use your time and energy in a more constructive way.

ASKING FORGIVENESS FOR *OUR* SINS

Let me make one final observation. In this chapter, we have talked primarily about our responsibility to confront family members and friends who sin against us and to seek reconciliation. However, there is another word from Jesus. It has to do with our own sin. His instructions are clear. "Therefore, if you are offering your gift at the altar and there remember that your brother has something against you [that is, you have wronged him], leave your gift there in front of the altar. First go and be reconciled to your brother; then come and offer your gift" (Matthew 5:23–24).

When we sin against others, it is our responsibility to confess and repent of our own sins. We should take the initiative as soon as we realize that we have done or said something unfairly to another. Thus, it will be clear to the astute reader that whether I have sinned against someone else or someone has sinned against me, it is my responsibility to take the initiative to seek reconciliation. If I have sinned against someone, very likely the person is experiencing anger toward me. If the person has sinned against me, then I am the one experiencing anger. Anger in God's economy is designed to motivate us to take constructive action in seeking to right the wrong and restore the fellowship with the other person.

THE PATH TO FORGIVENESS

When someone has caused your anger, and that anger is valid, based on a genuine transgression, reconciliation can come through forgiveness. The path to forgiveness has three markers.

First, rebuke the offending person, that is, bring the offense to the person's attention. The rebuke should be given in love, with the hope and willingness that forgiveness will result. Give the rebuke only after you have calmed emotionally.

Second, wait for the person to repent of his wrongdoing. He or she must repent. Such repentance includes confessing that the action was wrong and expressing a desire to turn from practicing that wrong in the future. When the individual does this, Jesus said we are to forgive the person.

Third, realize that some of the results of the sin will remain, even when forgiveness comes and the relationship is restored. The relationship may need time to heal, especially if a trust has been broken. Realize that you may be able to help the person to gradually move to a stronger relationship, but you may not fully erase the consequences. In some cases there are lasting social, emotional, or physical consequences. Among your emotions after you forgive may be disappointment or even anger every time you recall the event. Simply remember that forgiveness is not a feeling; it is an ongoing commitment to accept the person in spite of what he or she has done. Continue to forgive when such feelings arise.

FOR DISCUSSION

1. Injustice abounds in human society. Its effects on us vary with our proximity to the issue. A fraud scandal in Washington may make us angry at our government, but it's less likely to affect us as strongly as when a friend or family member betrays us. How does distance from the source of anger affect your ability to grant forgiveness to an offending party? How does the distance from the source of anger affect your ability to resolve your anger?

2. Repentance is an essential element in experiencing God's forgiveness. What must you do to repent when you have sinned before God? Discuss with group members some experience where you have asked for God's forgiveness. Did you always confess and repent of your wrongdoing? Did confession and repentance come easily? How did you sense God had forgiven you?

3. Human forgiveness should be modeled after divine forgiveness: confession and repentance by the sinning and forgiveness by the one sinned against. Share an experience with your group where you asked another person to forgive you. How does your experience compare or vary with God's requirement for forgiveness? Is it easier or harder to confess and repent to another person than to God? Why?

4. *Processing your anger:* You are the parents of a teenage son. For years you have lectured him on the dangers of alcohol and drugs, something he promised never to use. Today, you found out from the police that he was arrested for possession and use of a controlled substance. As you talk to him, you learn that he has been using drugs for over a year. How will you resolve your anger? How can you forgive your son?

Chapter 9

ANGER
IN
MARRIAGE

I don't ever remember losing my temper until I got married." Mike may have had a faulty memory about his years before marriage, but one thing he was certain of: Susan stimulated his anger. "When she says certain things or gives me *that* look, I get furious."

Upon further inquiry, I discovered that the comments that stimulated his anger were such things as "Are you going to mow the grass, or do I need to ask my father to come over and mow it?"; and "Do you think I am going to carry the garbage out after I've cooked the meal and washed the dishes? Shouldn't you take a little responsibility around here?"

Such rhetorical questions struck at the heart of Mike's self-esteem and stimulated defensive anger.

"That look" to which Mike referred was when Susan jerked her head to the right, set her eyes, and stared at him. "That look," he said, "is worse than a thousand condemning words. What I see in her eyes is, 'I'm sorry I married you.'"

Mike's interpretation of Susan's look revealed that his self-esteem was at the heart of his anger. Most of us want to be liked, accepted, and appreciated. When we get criticism, we tend to respond defensively. Susan may argue that she is criticizing Mike's behavior, not his person, but since our behavior is an extension of who we are, it is difficult for most of us, including Mike, to make the distinction. Mike's anger was stimulated because something deep within him said, "It is not right for her to put me down."

The tone of Susan's voice indicated that she too was angry. She has likely concluded that Mike is not doing his "fair share" around the house. The grass grows taller while he plays golf, and he watches television as she washes dishes and carries out the garbage. That is not exactly her idea of a loving husband.

All married couples experience anger. Experiencing anger is not wrong. The tragedy is that thousands of couples have never learned how to process anger productively. Thus, they explode in verbal tirades that do nothing but make the situation worse, or they suffer in isolated silence as they withdraw from each other. Most of us can look at our own childhood and remember picnics that were spoiled not by the rain but by the parents' anger toward each other. How many birthdays have been tainted by the bickering of parents who have not learned to resolve their anger? How many holidays have become days of horror because of the reign of anger?

Sadly, most married adults have never learned how to handle anger properly. Marriage becomes a battlefield, each spouse accusing the other of firing the first shot. If the couple do not learn to properly handle their anger, they will never have a satisfying marriage. I say "never" because love and uncontrolled anger cannot coexist. Love seeks the well-being of the spouse, while uncontrolled anger seeks to hurt and destroy.

STRATEGIES FOR HANDLING ANGER IN MARRIAGE

The good news is that couples can learn to handle anger responsibly. In fact, they must learn if they are to survive. I'm not suggesting that learning to handle anger is an easy process. I am suggesting that it is a necessary one, and any couple can be successful. Built upon the principles of anger management described in chapter 3, let me suggest a six-step strategy for handling anger in marriage.

First, acknowledge the reality of anger. In the course of marriage, each of us will experience anger from time to time. Some of this anger will be definitive, stimulated by wrong action on the part of the spouse. Some of this anger also will be distorted, stimulated by a misunderstanding of what happened. We will each experience a fair share of both types of anger. This is a part of being human and living life with each other. Remember, anger is not sinful; rather, it is evidence that we have a concern for fairness and justice. Thus, we do not need to condemn ourselves or each other for experiencing anger, nor do we need to deny that we are angry.

When we give each other the right to feel anger, we are giving each other the right to be human. This is the starting place in learning to process anger positively.

Second, agree to acknowledge your anger to each other. When you are angry with each other, give the other the benefit of knowing what you are feeling. Otherwise, the spouse must guess based on your behavior. Such "guessing games" are a waste of time and usually not very accurate. If you are angry toward your spouse, it's because he/she has done or said something that you deem inappropriate, or failed to do or say something that you expected. In your mind, your spouse has done you wrong. Your partner has treated you unkindly, unfairly, or inappropriately. You do not view the behavior as loving. At that moment, the event—the inappropriate action of your spouse—has become a barrier between the two of you. Your spouse deserves to know this. He cannot work on a problem of which he is unaware.

We each deserve the benefit of knowing when our spouse is angry and what she is angry about. The couple who commit to give each other this information has taken a major step in resolving anger productively.

Third, agree that verbal or physical explosions that attack the other person are not appropriate responses to anger. Such unhealthy venting of anger is always destructive and should not be accepted as appropriate behavior. This does not mean that once your spouse and you make this agreement neither of you will ever "lose your cool" again; however, it does mean that when you do so, you're committed to acknowledging that the response was wrong. Explosive expressions of anger always makes things worse, and the debris from such explosions must be cleared before we can deal constructively with the event that stimulated the original anger.

One practical way to break this negative practice of explosion is to agree that whenever either of you begins to explode, the other will walk out of the room, and if you are followed, you will walk out of the house. If the spouse pursues you in the yard with yelling and screaming, you will run to a neighbor's house or around the block. If you both agree to this strategy, then each of you will know that when the other starts walking or running, it's time to stop and reflect on what is happening. Hopefully when you return from the walk or run, your spouse will have calmed down and will be able to say, "I'm sorry. My exploding at you was wrong. I guess I was so hurt and angry I lost control. I'm sorry. Please forgive me." You can then forgive your spouse for this momentary lapse, and you can pursue the issue that originally stimulated his/her anger.

Fourth, agree to seek an explanation before passing judgment. If you are angry with your spouse, your first impression is that his behavior is wrong. But you should always take this as tentative until you hear his side. We often misinterpret the words and actions of our spouses. For instance, he forgot to bring the milk home even after he wrote himself a note. She interprets this as irresponsibility and she experiences anger. But it may be: the store was out of milk; he took a colleague home from the office and didn't go by the store; or he knew she didn't need the milk for dinner and plans to get it when he picks up Johnny from the ball game. If she is committed to seeking explanation, she will hold her judgment of irresponsibility as tentative until she hears his perspective.

Bob thought he heard his wife say on the telephone that he was "late and that she couldn't stand being late." He felt angry because he had made every effort to be there on time and was only two minutes late. When he sought an explanation, he found that she was actually talking about a friend's baby who arrived two weeks late. If actions and words are open to misunderstanding, motives are even more difficult. Since motives are internal, we can never know another person's motives unless they tell us. We often attribute motives to our spouse that are totally off base.

Jonathan was acting wisely when he said: "I may really be misreading this and that's why I'm asking for an explanation. It appears to me that you wrote a check for $300 to the department store. I thought we agreed that neither of us would spend over $100 without consulting the other until we get our debts under control." He was shocked by Bethany's response.

"Oh, Darling, I can explain. Our section at work went together and bought Betsy a retirement gift. They asked me to pick it up during my lunch hour since I was meeting Ginger at the mall. So I wrote a check for the whole thing, but they each gave me $20. It's in my purse. I think I have $300. If so, my part is only the tax."

Jonathan's anger subsided as he counted the $300. Then he smiled as he remembered what his response would have been six months ago, before he and Bethany took a marriage enrichment class and learned how to process anger. He could visualize his face getting red and his voice exploding to Bethany about what she had done.

"I really am making progress," he said aloud.

"What are you talking about?" Bethany asked.

"I was just thinking about how I would have responded before we took the marriage enrichment class." Jonathan was smiling now. "I would have been furious and would not have asked for an explanation. Then I would have felt stupid afterwards when you told me what happened. I much prefer our new system." Jonathan and Bethany have learned the benefit of seeking an explanation before making final judgments.

Fifth, agree to seek a resolution. In the case of Jonathan and Bethany, Jonathan's anger was resolved once he received Bethany's explanation. Obviously not all anger resolution is that easy. Let's assume that Bethany had actually broken their commitment and had made a $300 purchase after agreeing that neither of them would purchase anything over $100 without discussing it with the other. Let's assume her explanation was, "But, Honey, it was on sale. I saved $200 and we need it. I didn't think you would object."

"Well, I do object," Jonathan replies. "It would be nice to have it, but we don't really need it. We've gotten along quite well without it, and we cannot afford to add $300 to our debt. We made an agreement and you have broken the agreement. And I think that is wrong."

Bethany replies, "I'm surprised at your response. I really didn't think that you would object. I thought you wanted it as much as I did."

"I do want it, Sweetheart. I would like to have it, but we cannot afford it. And we agreed to draw the line on purchases and I think we must stick to our agreement."

"Well, if you insist. I can take it back," Bethany says. "I don't want to but I will."

"It's not a matter of wanting," said Jonathan. His voice is firm but not loud. He is in control of his feelings and offers an explanation. "I would like to keep it, but the bottom line is we can't afford it now. I wish we could, but you know our situation as well as I do."

"OK," said Bethany. "Then I'll take it back."

"Fine. You do know that I love you and someday we will buy it," adds Jonathan, putting his hand on her shoulder.

"I know you love me, Darling, and in retrospect it was a poor decision. I'm glad you are holding me to our agreement."

Some of you are asking, "Is that not extremely idealistic?" My response is,

"Not for couples who have learned how to process anger responsibly and who are committed to loving each other."

Sixth, agree to affirm your love for each other. After the anger is resolved, tell each other of your love. In doing so you are saying, "I am not going to allow this event to separate us." As a couple, you have heard each other out, the issue has been resolved, you have learned from the experience, and you move on together.

Where genuine wrong has been committed, where one has been unkind, unloving, or unjust, resolution requires confession and repentance on the part of the one who committed the indiscretion and forgiveness on the part of the other. Anger subsides when this process has been completed. Anger has served its noble purpose of holding each of us accountable for our behavior.

In the case of distorted anger, where the anger is stimulated by a perceived wrong that later turns out to be a misunderstanding, resolution comes by means of seeking explanation and finding that one's original interpretation of events was wrong. The person who has not learned the difference between definitive anger and distorted anger will assume that his anger is always legitimate and the other person's actions always wrong. Such an assumption does not allow anger to be resolved and will, in fact, stimulate anger in the spouse who knows that your anger is distorted. Your rigid insistence on being right will stimulate anger in your spouse which also needs to be resolved.

One can easily understand how unresolved anger can snowball and become an ever-increasing problem as the marriage goes on. Few things are more important to a successful marriage than learning to resolve anger in a responsible manner.

I believe a genuine commitment to these six principles will get a couple on the pathway toward productive anger management. Marriages need not be destroyed by uncontrolled anger. The Christian must set the pace in learning how to handle anger responsibly. It is my sincere desire that this book will help thousands of couples come to grips with what has become a major problem in Christian marriages. If you are married, I urge you to mutually commit yourself to these six principles and begin today to practice them.

GETTING STARTED

In my efforts to help couples get started, I have often suggested the following exercise. On a three-by-five card, write the following words: "I'm feeling angry right now but don't worry, I'm not going to attack you. But I do need your help. Is this a good time to talk?" Put this card on the refrigerator door or some other easily accessible place. The next time you feel anger toward your spouse, run for the card. (A detachable card with these words appears at the back of this book.) Holding it in your hand, read it to your spouse as calmly as you can. If it's not "a good time to talk," then set a time to talk. And at the appointed time, begin the process of seeking explanation and resolution of the issue that stimulated your anger. In this brief written speech, you have acknowledged that you are experiencing anger, you have affirmed your commitment not to explode, and you have expressed your desire for explanation and resolution through conversation.

When you sit down to discuss the issue, begin by saying, "I know that I could be misunderstanding this and that's why I wanted to talk with you. Let me tell you what I am feeling and why. Then if you can clarify the situation, please do so because I need help in resolving this." Such a beginning creates a nonthreatening atmosphere in which to discuss the event that stimulated your anger.

In every marriage, anger will make its occasional visit for reasons discussed throughout this book. I believe that anger is a friend, not an enemy. The Christian couple who understands the source of anger and the purpose of anger has also the aid of the Holy Spirit to practice this disciplined biblical approach to resolving anger in a constructive manner. This lesson is one of the most important you will ever learn and is an essential ingredient to a successful marriage. Learning to resolve your anger in a positive way will also have a profound effect upon the lives of your children, which brings us to chapter 10: "Teaching Children to Handle Anger."

DEALING WITH ANGER TOWARD YOUR SPOUSE

*H*ere are six steps for dealing with anger you feel toward your spouse. Most of these six steps should be in place before the anger comes; that way, when it appears, an agreed-upon plan can help calm and direct the discussion.

1. *Acknowledge the reality of anger.* Whether your anger is legitimate, definitive anger or distorted anger, do not condemn yourself for experiencing anger. Recognize and admit to it, remembering the anger itself is not sinful.

2. *Agree to acknowledge your anger to each other.* Express clearly your feeling of anger when it arises; do not make your spouse guess based on your behavior. Both you and your spouse deserve to know when the other is angry and what he or she is angry about.

3. *Agree that verbal or physical explosions against the other person are not appropriate responses to anger.* Either kind of explosion will always make things worse.

4. *Agree to seek an explanation before passing judgment.* Remember that your first impression is only tentative; at times it will be faulty. It is easy to misinterpret the words and actions of one's spouse, so seek your mate's perspective. He or she may supply valuable missing information that could change your understanding of the issue.

5. *Agree to seek a resolution.* With more information from your spouse and the fuller perspective, you are ready to find a solution satisfactory to both of you. Resolving the angry feelings may require that you seek the person's confession and repentance—if the wrongdoing is valid and definitive—or recognize your anger as invalid and perhaps selfish —if the anger is distorted. It may require even confession and asking of forgiveness on your part, if the wrongdoing is by you. Whatever the cause, work toward a reconciliation between the two of you.

6. *Agree to affirm your love for each other.* After the anger is resolved, declare verbally your love for each other.

FOR DISCUSSION

1. A marriage relationship is a very fertile field for anger to develop and blossom. Anger's harmful effects are particularly profound in marriage due to the intimate nature of a couple's bond to one another. List five things that your spouse does or has done that anger you. The items might be as trivial as not hanging up a coat routinely to a major issue such as lying. Have these issues been resolved? Is one or both spouses still angry?

2. Review the six-step strategy for handling anger in marriage, summarized on the facing page. Within your group, develop an anger in marriage scenario such as excessive spending by one spouse. Discuss each step and how you would implement some action in resolving your anger or your spouse's anger.

3. How does the six-step strategy work in cases of distorted anger? Create another scenario in which one spouse's anger is created by distorted facts or circumstances, such as a spouse who spends too much time at work, leading the other spouse to imagine work is more important than the spouse. Does the process or resolution change?

4. *Processing your anger:* You have been married five years. You regularly experience anger toward your spouse because he/she is less outgoing than you are and dislikes attending parties and social gatherings. You sense that your friends are "having all the fun" while you are "wasting away at home." How can you resolve your anger?

Chapter 10

TEACHING CHILDREN TO HANDLE ANGER

*R*achel, a single mom, is trying to prepare Sunday lunch. Meanwhile, six-year-old Megan and eight-year-old Robert are playing in the den. At least Rachel thought they were playing; suddenly it sounds more like warfare than play. As Rachel walks in the den, she sees Robert hit his sister across the back with a stuffed bear. Megan begins to cry.

"She stole my book," Robert says.

"I did not," Megan insists.

Rachel grabs Robert by the arm, plants a solid blow to his buttocks and says, "Go to your room and don't come out till I call you." Then she turns to Megan and says, "How many times have I told you not to mess with your brother's things?"

"I didn't," Megan says. "I was just trying to get on the couch and he hit me."

"I don't want to hear it," Rachel says. "I can't even get lunch ready without you two fighting. You go to your room and I'll call you when lunch is ready."

"You always blame me," Megan says as she walks to her room.

Rachel knows something went wrong, but she isn't sure how to correct it. As parents, we must remember that children experience anger similar to our own. Their anger can be stimulated by injustice, or it can be distorted. Perhaps Megan did Robert wrong, but his response was not healthy. It is obvious that Megan not only felt her brother's action was unjustified, but also that her mother's judgment was unfair. Rachel's response to her own anger did not effectively teach her children how to manage their anger.

Few parental responsibilities are more important than teaching your children how to handle anger constructively. However, many parents feel ill-equipped to teach about managing anger. When we observe our children having what we consider to be inappropriate responses to anger, we often panic and respond negatively, thus missing an opportunity to train our children. Having been such a panic-stricken parent, I write this chapter with great empathy for parents who are still struggling with this parental responsibility.

The reality is all children will experience anger. We don't have to teach children to experience anger. Our task is to teach them how to manage their anger. Because of the nature of the parent-child relationship, parents are the most influential persons in developing a child's pattern of anger management. This should encourage us, because it gives us an opportunity to give our children positive anger management skills. On the other hand, this can be a frightening reality, because if we fail in this area, our children will be disadvantaged as they move to adulthood.

As I talk to parents across the country, most are eager to learn how to help their children in this important area of development. Let me share with you the principles I have shared with many parents in the counseling room and in parenting workshops. They are simple to understand but not necessarily easy to do. Putting these principles in practice will require not only your best attention, but also the aid of the Holy Spirit. The good news is that when we are seeking to follow biblical principles, the Spirit's help is readily available.

THE FOUNDATION OF LOVE

Let me begin with what I believe to be foundational: *Focus on meeting your child's need for emotional love.* Why am I bringing up the subject of love when we are talking about anger? Because love is the foundation for healthy parent-child relationships. If the child does not feel loved by the parent, not only will the child experience greater anger, but all efforts on the part of the parent to teach the child are likely to be rejected. In *The Five Love Languages of Children*, which I coauthored with psychiatrist Ross Campbell, I emphasize the importance of meeting the child's need for love. If the child's emotional love tank is not filled with parental love, the empty tank will itself become a source of anger. Something deep within the heart of each child is constantly saying, "Parents are supposed to love children." If the child does not feel that love, there is a sense of being treated unfairly, and this gives rise to anger.

The five love languages—words of affirmation, quality time, gifts, acts of service, and physical touch—need to be spoken to children regularly. Every child has one primary love language that clearly communicates love to him. As parents, we can love our children most effectively by discovering their primary love language and speaking it even more frequently than the other four.

Let me emphasize that such expressions of love must be unconditional. Many parents without realizing it give love only when their children are in a pleasant mood or doing what the parents desire. These parents think that if they withhold expressions of love, their children will do what they desire. This almost never happens. When it does, the child is almost always rebelling inside.

Parents need not be pleased with the child's behavior in order to give the child a hug, a pat on the back, or an affirming arm on the shoulder. Parents can say, "You played a great game last night," even though the child's room may be a disaster area. A dad can take a son out to breakfast for quality time even when the son broke the rule and vase by bouncing the basketball in the den. A mother can give a daughter a new dress as a gift even though the daughter did not complete her homework. "But won't this cause my children to be irresponsible?" many parents ask. The answer is, "Such love teaches responsibility." When the child senses that you love her and that love is not based on her behavior, she is far more likely to be responsive to your requests or your commands and to do so without rebellion. When you love your children unconditionally and keep the love tank full, you have removed one of the major sources of childhood and adolescent anger.[1]

The message our children need to hear and feel is, "I love you no matter what you do. I don't always like what you do nor agree with what you do, but I will always love you." Children who feel the security of parental love are much more likely to make wise choices in life; and when they do make poor choices, they are far more likely to learn from their mistakes and to correct future behavior. Nothing is more fundamental in teaching a child to handle anger than giving the child unconditional love.

Let me emphasize that a child's need for love is continuous. Love is like food; it cannot be stored up—it needs to be expressed daily. We do not fill our children's love tank and then take a vacation. The love tank empties quickly as does the stomach. The wise parent will discover the child's primary love language and give heavy doses daily, sprinkling in the other four regularly.

With this foundation laid, I believe there are three primary methods whereby we teach our children how to handle their anger positively. I want to discuss them in what I believe to be the order of importance, but I want to emphasize that all of these methods are important; none of them can be omitted. I believe that by giving attention to these three methods, any parent can teach their children positive anger management.

BEING A MODEL

Scott and Dee are parents of Matt, age fourteen, and Missy, age eighteen. They are sitting in my office on a beautiful October afternoon. The white clouds are floating through the blue Carolina sky, and the brilliant yellow leaves outside my window are dancing in the breeze. However, Scott and Dee are not looking at the clouds or the leaves; their eyes focus on my gray carpet. Scott begins their story.

"Dr. Chapman, we feel like a failure with our son. Our daughter never caused us any problems, but we've always had struggles with our son. The main problem is his anger. This year has been the worst. Maybe it's because he is a teenager now."

"It's like he doesn't respect us," Dee adds. "He screams at me all the time; everything I do is wrong. And now he's started screaming at his father. We have got to have help."

With that information, I began a dialogue with the parents. "How do you typically respond to Matt's yelling and screaming?" I asked Scott.

"Well, usually I'm calm and I try to listen to him and reason with him. But after awhile, he becomes so illogical that I lose my cool and end up yelling at him. I know that's not right, but it's like I don't know what else to do."

"And how do you typically respond?" I asked Dee.

"We've always screamed at each other," she said. "I don't think he should be allowed to talk to us that way. I scream at Matt and when he leaves, I scream at Scott. I tell him that he shouldn't let Matt talk to us that way. I'm a wreck. Maybe I'm the one who needs help."

Dee's openness so early in our conversation surprised me. I could tell that she was desperate. She wasn't playing games. She sincerely wanted help.

"I'm glad you have come today. I believe the first step is always reaching out for help. I want to assure you that a lot of other couples have struggled with similar situations, and I believe that there are answers. But I want to begin by asking you a few questions which may seem to be unrelated but I think will help us get a perspective on things. OK?"

They agreed, and I began by asking Scott to recall his childhood and tell me how his parents handled anger in their relationship.

"My father was the angry one," he said. "I don't mean he was angry all the time. He was basically a good man, but once in awhile he would lose his temper and yell at Mom or me," he said.

"And how did you and your mom respond to his yelling?"

"We both clammed up," he said. "When Dad started yelling, we knew there was no need to respond. I think Mom had learned that it would simply escalate matters. So if he got loud, she got silent, and that's basically what I did. Dad would sputter on for awhile and then walk out of the room. And the next day, he acted like nothing had ever happened. It was never brought up again. Fortunately, this didn't happen too often, so most of my childhood was rather calm and good."

"What about your home, Dee? How did your parents handle anger?"

She smiled and said, "I grew up in an Italian home. We were always loud. Everybody screamed at everybody but when it was over, it was over. Nobody carried a grudge; everybody had their say and it was finished."

"I want to make an observation," I said. "Scott, I think I remember you saying that typically in your response to Matt, you tend to be quiet but after awhile, you lose your temper and yell back at him. Is that correct?"

"Yes," he said, nodding his head. "So typically you respond to Matt's yelling in the same way you and your mother responded to your father's yelling? Is that correct?"

"Yes, except that eventually I start yelling at Matt. I never did that with my father."

"And, Dee, if I heard you correctly, you said that you and Matt have always screamed at each other, which is pretty much like it was in your childhood home."

"Yes, except that Matt never stops. It's never over with Matt."

"The reason I ask these question," I said, "is because most of us learn how to manage anger by observing our parents handle anger. And typically, we identify with the parent whose personality is most like ours. I haven't asked this, Scott, but I'm guessing that your personality is more like your mother than your father; is that correct?"

"Definitely," he said.

"So your most basic response to anger is to be silent. It's only after you are pushed to the limit that you explode and become like your father. Your parents had two very different ways of handling anger. Your mother withdrew in silence and your father yelled and screamed. So you had two models. You identified most closely with your mother but on occasion, you responded like your father.

"Dee, apparently in your house your mother and father yelled at each other when angry. That was their way of processing their anger. So as an adult, that is the method you typically follow. The difference in your marriage, of course, is that most of the time, Scott does not yell back; he becomes silent and so you have your say while he sits in silence."

"Yes, and that makes me even madder," Dee said. "I wish he would yell back at me."

"And yet, if I understood you correctly, you don't want Matt to yell at you."

"Matt is different," she said. "He's our child; he's not my husband. Children shouldn't yell at parents."

"Did you yell at your parents?" I asked. Dee was silent for a moment and then said, "Yes, I guess I did."

Dee and Scott are illustrating the profound effect of the parental model. Perhaps without ever talking about it, each of their parents taught them a method of responding to anger. Now as adults, that is the method each of them uses. By their own admission, it's not a very effective method. Now in their efforts to teach Matt how to handle anger, they are consciously seeking new information as to how they might process their own anger in a more constructive way.

Many parents can identify with Dee and Scott. Often adults do not consciously think of their own anger management until they observe their children's response to anger. Many times, children mirror what they have learned from parents. Typically, as in the case of Matt, children respond to anger much in the same way as the parent whose personality is most like their own. Since Matt was a child, when Dee was angry with his behavior, she had expressed her anger in loud verbal tirades toward him. Matt now expresses his anger in a similar way.

Fortunately, adults can learn to change destructive patterns and establish new and healthier models of processing anger. Through several sessions, I worked with Dee and Scott, helping them understand the ideas we have shared in this book and watching them learn how to share their anger with each other in an open, loving, non-condemning manner. On occasion, Matt observed them talking and listening to each other as they discussed the issues that stimulated their anger. He told me later, "I knew something strange was going on but I didn't know what. I had never heard them talk that openly to each other without screaming."

Later on, Dee and Scott told Matt about what had happened: They had realized that their model of handling anger was not very positive and had decided to go for counseling; they were learning new ways to respond to their own anger. Matt seemed pleased, although he didn't say much at the moment. They knew, however, that he was getting the message when one night as Dee was getting a bit tense, Matt said, "Mom, I think you need to get the three-by-five card and read it to Dad." Dee said, "I think you're right, Matt. Thanks."

They were really shocked one night about two months later when Matt walked into the room holding the three-by-five card and said, "I'm feeling angry right now but don't worry, I'm not going to attack you. But I do need your help. Is this a good time to talk?" They both broke into laughter. Matt smiled and said, "No, guys, I'm really serious. I'm angry and I need to talk with you about it." They switched off the TV, gave Matt their undivided attention, and for the first time allowed Matt to process his anger following the model they had set.

Most children will respond positively when they become aware that their parents have acknowledged that their method of handling anger needs to be improved. When they see actual changes taking place, it enhances their sense of security and will begin to have a positive impact upon their own anger management.

GIVING GUIDANCE

Parents who take seriously their responsibility to teach their children to process anger positively can help a second way: Choose to take an active role in guiding the children through their own anger episodes. The parent recognizes that children cannot be expected to handle anger in a mature manner until they have been taught. Just as a child must be taught how to wash dishes, make up a bed, and ride a bicycle, so a child must be taught how to handle anger. This involves accepting the child's present level of development and helping him make steps in growth.

A child has only two basic ways to express anger: verbally and behaviorally. Each of these can be positive or negative. Behaviorally, a child may express anger by pushing, shoving, striking, throwing objects, pulling hair, or beating his own head against the wall. Obviously, these are negative behavioral responses to anger. On the other hand, leaving the room, counting to 100 aloud, taking a walk around the block are mature behavioral responses to anger that allow the child to cool down and process anger in a constructive manner.

On the verbal side, the child may yell and scream condemning statements, may use profanity or name-calling—all very destructive ways of verbalizing anger. On the other hand, the extremely mature child may acknowledge to the parent that he is angry and ask for an opportunity to discuss his complete concerns. That is a very positive way of verbally expressing anger. The task of the parent is to take the child where he is and help him move toward more constructive ways of processing anger.

Some parents have difficulty accepting a child's limits and imperfections in managing his anger. They want the child to be mature in his expressions of anger and are unwilling to allow the stages of immaturity. The parent who says, "Shut up. You're not going to talk to me that way. Don't ever raise your voice at me again. Do you understand?" is expecting perfection from the child. This is unrealistic. In fact, the parent is expecting of the child a level of maturity that the parent has not attained. As one young man said to me, "My parents yell and scream at me, telling me not to yell and scream at them."

If your child is screaming at you in anger, listen! Calmly ask questions and let the anger be expressed. The more questions you ask and the more intently you listen, the more likely his volume will decrease. Concentrate on the reason your child is angry, not on the way he is expressing it. Seek to understand what he thinks is unfair or wrong. You may not agree with his perception, but the purpose is to hear him out. If he thinks he was wronged, the anger will not go away until he feels that you have heard and understood his complaint. You are the parent and you have the final word on what will be done, but your child needs to feel that you think his feelings and ideas are important. Don't let the child's method of delivering his message keep you from getting the message.

After you have had a "listening session" with an angry child, later that night or the next day you might say, "I really appreciate your sharing with me your anger about that situation. We may not always agree, but I want you to know that I always want to understand how you feel. I'm not a perfect parent and sometimes I don't make the best decision. But I really want to do what is best for you. I hope that we can both learn how to express our feelings more calmly, but however they are expressed, I always want to hear how you feel and think."

If your pattern has been one of arguing with your child, perhaps you can break the pattern by saying, "I've been thinking about us and I have realized that I am not a very good listener. Usually when you are feeling strongly about something, I also end up getting heated. I really want to be a better listener. In the future, I am going to try to ask more questions and really seek to understand your feelings, because I really do value your ideas and your feelings." As parents become better listeners, their children feel more understood. The child still may not agree with your final decision, but your son will respect you because you have treated him as a person. If you listen and ask questions calmly, in time your daughter will learn to process her anger in a more conversational tone, and your shouting matches will be a thing of the past.

If your child is using some of the negative behavioral responses to anger, such as pushing, shoving, and throwing objects, focus on the anger first and the behavior second. You might say, "It's obvious that you are very angry. I would like to hear what's bothering you but we can't talk while you are _____. Would you like for us to take a walk and talk about it?" What you are doing with such an approach is acknowledging the importance of the child's anger and expressing a desire to discuss the issues that concern him while acknowledging in a kind but firm way that you cannot talk until the destructive behavior ends.

Many times the parent's anger is stirred by the child's behavior, and the parent responds to the child in an equally destructive manner. Eventually, both feel badly about their behavior but nothing is done to resolve the issue that originally stimulated the child's anger. Obviously, the parent and the child have a great deal to learn about anger management. I do not intend to convey that what I am suggesting is easy to do. Parents who have never learned to control their own anger may find it hard to imagine taking the approach I am suggesting. But consider this:

- The child by virtue of being a child is immature. She is still in process. Thus, her anger management is not yet mature.

- Parents are older and at least have had time to be more mature. If we have not developed a mature response to anger, let's at least admit that it is our problem and not our child's problem.

When we parents learn to handle our own anger in a healthier manner, we will then be in a position to guide our children in processing their anger. Children desperately need our parental guidance.

An angry child needs to be heard, because in his mind the parents have treated him unfairly, embarrassed him, disappointed him, or in some way treated him unjustly. If parents do not hear the child's complaints and seek to understand why the child feels this, the child's anger will be internalized and later show up in the child's behavior. Psychologists call this passive-aggressive behavior. The child is passive on the outside, but inside the anger is growing and will eventually express itself in aggressive behavior, such as low grades, drug experimentation, sexual activity, "forgetting" to do homework, or some other behavior that the child knows will upset the parent. If parents understood the extreme danger of passive-aggressive behavior, they would make every effort to listen to their children when they are angry, to hear the issues carefully, to seek to understand, and find a resolution.

This does not mean that the parent must always do what the child is requesting. The child's anger is often distorted, that is, rooted in a perceived wrong rather than a definitive wrong. An explanation from the parent may bring resolution. The important thing is that the child feels that you are genuinely concerned and that your action reflects your genuine love for him.

Each anger experience gives the parent an opportunity to guide the child through the angry episode, deal with the issues, and find a resolution. Each time this is done, the child becomes a bit more mature in verbalizing her anger. There is less need for yelling and screaming because the parents are listening intently and the child is assured that she is being heard. Such parental guidance is an extremely effective way of teaching children to handle anger responsibly.

GIVING INSTRUCTION

Most parents want to *start* with giving instructions. "Let me tell you some things you need to know," they may begin. Without question, most parents know a great deal that their children need to learn, and instruction can be an effective method of communicating. Give instruction. But be sure the foundation of love has been set; such unconditional love provides part of a rich soil for growing a child's heart. If the heart of the child has not been cultivated by unconditional love, positive modeling, and loving guidance on the part of parents, the seed of instruction is not likely to grow. However, if these are in place and the child's heart has been cultivated, then instruction is an excellent method of teaching a child how to handle anger.

There are many methods and places for parents to give verbal instruction to children about matters related to anger. Depending on the age of the child, the following are effective ways of helping a child understand and process anger effectively.

For the young child, reading and discussing Bible stories that focus on anger provide an interesting format for instructing children. Such stories as Cain and Abel, Joseph and his eleven brothers, Jonah and his anger toward God, Jesus and His anger toward the money changers all provide key insights into understanding anger. Reading the wisdom found in the book of Proverbs provides excellent instruction in how to handle anger. Many of the proverbs relate specifically to anger management.

Memorizing key Scriptures is an excellent method of instruction for young children. Consider these verses, all from Proverbs: "A fool gives full vent to his anger, but a wise man keeps himself under control." "An angry man stirs up dissension, and a hot-tempered one commits many sins." "A quick-tempered man does foolish things." "A patient man has great understanding, but a quick-tempered man displays folly" (29:11, 22; 14:17, 29). Printing these verses on cards and memorizing them with your children is planting seeds of wisdom in their mind and yours. Another great verse for your child to memorize is Ephesians 4:26–27: 'In your anger do not sin': Do not let the sun go down while you are still angry, and do not give the devil a foothold."

For older children, reading and discussing this book could be an excellent way of giving instruction on understanding and processing anger. Encouraging a child to write a research paper on the topic of anger is another way of instruction. Such research could involve not only reading books and perhaps searching the Internet, but also interviewing parents and grandparents for ideas on the source of anger and how to process anger constructively. This could be an exciting project for the teenager or older child.

Informal conversation is also an excellent way for a parent to instruct a child regarding managing his anger. For the older child, such an open conversation, allowing the child to ask questions and make comments, could be a springboard not only for discussing anger as a topic but also for discussing how the two of you have processed anger in the past and what positive changes might be made. In such a family conversation, parents might share with a child their own struggles with anger both as children and as a married couple. Such openness on the part of parents creates an atmosphere for the child or teenager to express his or her own struggles or to ask questions.

Such conversations can easily be initiated by sharing with the child something you read recently. For example, "I was reading an article the other day on anger. It said that many parents are not aware of how many times they lose their temper with their children and say things that actually hurt the children; the parent never remembers what he said. I was wondering if that could possibly be true of me." "Well, Mom, since you brought it up ..."

When you make your anger the focus of the conversation rather than the child's anger, you make it easier for the child to be responsive and reveal his perceptions of you and the way you handle anger. Such conversations can be extremely instructive to a child and may also bring insight to the parent.

In teaching our child, it's important that we not come across as having the final answer to everything related to anger. The child knows better than that —she has been living with you for several years now. Far better to be honest that you realize that you are still in process, that you want to do better at managing your anger and at the same time, you want to understand her concerns when she is angry. The child is usually willing to "cut the parents some slack" so long as the parent does not come across with a "know-it-all" attitude.

Children are usually willing to forgive us for failures in managing our own anger if we are willing to confess our failures. "I'm sorry, Son, that I lost my temper this afternoon. I didn't handle my anger very well, and the way I talked to you was not kind, and some of the things I said are not really the way I feel. I want you to know that I recognize that was wrong and I have asked God to forgive me; and I want to ask you to forgive me." Such an honest confession will go a long way toward creating respect in the heart of the child. Children already know that what we did was wrong. If we do not confess, their respect for us is diminished. When we confess, their respect is restored. In responsibly handling our failures, we are teaching children not only what is right and wrong about anger; we are also teaching them how to confess their failures when they mismanage their own anger.

For parents who feel the need for additional instruction in this topic, I highly recommend Ross Campbell's book *Kids in Danger: Training Your Child to Tame the Destructive Power of Anger* (Chariot/Victor). This book includes sections on passive-aggressive behavior and children with special problems such as Attention Deficit Disorder and Attention Deficit Hyperactive Disorder.

A positive parental model, loving parental guidance, and non-condemning instruction are in my opinion the most powerful approaches to teaching your children positive anger management.

NOTE

1. For further information on how to meet your child's need for emotional love, see Gary Chapman and Ross Campbell, *The Five Love Languages of Children* (Chicago: Northfield, 1997).

TEACHING YOUR CHILDREN
TO DEAL WITH ANGRY FEELINGS

*T*here are three primary methods whereby we can teach our children how to handle their anger positively. The three ways are mentioned in order of importance, though all are necessary.

First, model proper behavior. Children will imitate behavior and responses they observe in their parents. Children respond to anger in much the same way as the parent whose personality is most like their own. If a parent has destructive patterns, the adult can learn new, healthier responses to anger. When children see in their parents actual positive changes toward anger, it enhances their sense of security and will begin to have a positive impact upon their own anger management.

Second, take an active role in guiding the children through their own anger episodes. Begin at the child's present level of development and help him take steps in growth. Be sure to listen to the child, so that you can understand what he thinks is unfair or wrong. As the parent, you have the final word on what will be done, but your child needs to feel that you think his feelings and ideas are important. Be careful not to let the child's behavior stir your anger so that you respond to the child in an equally destructive manner. Each anger experience gives the parent an opportunity to guide the child through the anger episode, deal with the issues, and find a resolution.

Third, give instruction. Your instruction must be founded in the soil of unconditional love, positive modeling, and loving guidance.

FOR DISCUSSION

1. Children experience anger much like adults but generally lack the maturity and knowledge to handle it effectively. What things can you do with children to help them understand anger? How can you communicate with children to improve the way they respond to their own anger?

2. Recall the three methods we can teach children how to handle anger effectively: (1) model effectively; (2) take an active role in guiding the children through their own anger episodes; and (3) give instruction. Within the group, discuss the role parents should play in each of these teaching methods. Why is the parent's role so pivotal in shaping a child's ability to handle anger? How important is it for both parents to be involved in the teaching/mentoring process?

3. From the discussion on children learning by our model, you can see how important it is to be constant role models for our children. When your children display explosive forms of anger, should you attribute this behavior to the child or yourself? Or others? Who or what is the child's role model and how is this affecting the child? Discuss within the group the importance of listening to the child express his or her anger. What can you learn from listening? What does the child learn from your listening to him/her?

4. *Processing your anger:* You are the parent of two daughters, ages eleven and thirteen. Both girls are ordinarily well behaved, but can be intensely jealous of one another. The younger girl does her chores around the house with little prompting, but the older girl requires more supervision and frequently forgets to perform her assigned tasks. On occasion, due to differing circumstances, you have excused the older girl from her chores. Although the reasons for exempting the older girl seem reasonable to you, your younger daughter is very upset at the situation. She exhibits her anger both at you and at her sister with ugly comments and temper tantrums. The older sister returns the anger and behavior. How can you resolve this situation?

Chapter 11

WHEN YOU ARE ANGRY WITH GOD

*E*dna was past the weeping stage when she sat in my office, but she was red hot with anger. Jennifer, her eldest child and only daughter, had been killed three months earlier by a drunken driver. The shock, the hurt, and the unmitigated pain had seemed almost unbearable to Edna. Now as she came out of shock into the world of painful reality, she was grieving over her tragic loss, and her loss was compounded by her anger.

Anger and grief are often companions in such situations. Edna was angry at the drunken driver who killed her daughter. She was angry with the judicial system which had allowed him on the road again after three DUI convictions, and she was angry with her estranged husband who had bought Jennifer "that little car." "She didn't stand a chance in that little car," Edna said. "It was a death trap."

As I continued to listen as Edna shared her thoughts and feelings, I felt deep empathy. I also knew that Edna's talking with me was a positive step in processing her grief and anger. Wanting to discover the focus of her anger and knowing that Edna was a deeply committed Christian, I asked, "What are your feelings toward God in all of this?"

"I hate to say this, Dr. Chapman, but to be honest, I'm mad at God right now. I feel like He has deserted me. He could have spared Jennifer's life. She was so young and talented. Why would God allow this? I don't understand."

Christians often experience anger toward God in the face of tragedy. Often the stronger one's Christian commitment, the more intense will be the person's anger toward God. As Edna said later, "I've tried to live for God and be faithful. Why would He let this happen to me?" Edna was experiencing what Job must have experienced, for he too was "a righteous man." (See Job 1:8; 2:3.) When God allowed Job to lose his wealth, his family, and his health, this righteous man felt intense anger toward God. Job said, "God has turned me over to evil men and thrown me into the clutches of the wicked." He lost his desire to live. "Only a few years will pass before I go on the journey of no return. My spirit is broken, my days are cut short, the grave awaits me. . . . My days have passed, my plans are shattered, and so are the desires of my heart" (Job 16:11, 22; 17:1, 11). Job did not understand any better than Edna why God would allow such tragedy into his life, and he was clearly angry with God.

HOW GOD FEELS TOWARD OUR ANGER

When we look at Job and other biblical examples of people who were angry with God, it is clear that God did not condemn such anger. Rather, He entered into conversation with these people and helped them work through their anger. However, this does not mean that He always gave a full explanation of why bad things happened to good people. The book of Job is a long discourse between Job and his "friends" and between Job and God. His friends essentially accused Job of having done wrong and claimed the tragedy was God's judgment for his sin. Job insisted that this was not the case.

After listening sympathetically to Job's expressions of anger toward God, God's response was not one of condemnation. God reminded Job that His ways were not always understandable to men. He reminded Job that He is the all-powerful Creator and Sustainer of all that is and that in the final analysis, He is a God of justice who can be trusted.[1] In the end, God expressed His own anger toward Job's friends for condemning him and urged them to repent of their wrongdoing and ask Job to pray for them. "My servant Job will pray for you, and I will accept his prayer and not deal with you according to your folly" (Job 42:8).

Job's ultimate response was to trust God even though he did not understand. Through this experience, Job's relationship with God deepened. In his own words, "My ears had heard of you but now my eyes have seen you." The

Scriptures then record that "the Lord blessed the latter part of Job's life more than the first" (Job 42:5, 12).

"WHY DID GOD NOT DO SOMETHING?"

Clearly, God is sympathetic with His people as they pass through grief and anger. He is fully willing to hear our expressions of anger and to listen as we pour out our pain. It is not sinful to feel angry toward God. It is human. We have a concern for righteousness and whenever we encounter what we perceive to be unjust events, we experience anger. Knowing that God is all-powerful and could have averted these events, our anger is often toward God. "Why did God not do something?" is a question hurting Christians often ask. Theologically, we know that God does no wrong, but emotionally we experience anger.

When I ponder this question, two alternatives come to mind, for clearly God can do something. One, God could eliminate all sinful people and thus wipe out all the pain caused by their sinful acts. This, however, would eliminate the entire human race, because the Bible says, "All have sinned" (Romans 3:23). The second possibility would be for God to step in and miraculously avert the consequences of all evil. God could stop all bombs from exploding, stall all cars of drunken drivers, eliminate all germs and viruses, still all storms, exterminate all fires as soon as the spark ignites, evaporate all bullets, strike mute all who begin to speak a hurtful word, bring temporary blindness upon all stalkers and all who look with lustful thoughts. While this may sound inviting, it removes man's freedom and makes of him a robot who must do only good deeds. Apparently God values freedom, and freedom requires the option to disobey as well as to obey. There can be no freedom without the possibility of evil, and evil always has negative consequences.

In addition to the injustices caused by evil, Christians often struggle with the apparent personal inequities they endure. "Why did my son die with cancer when others less righteous than he continue to live? . . . Why did my spouse die at an early age while my godless neighbor continues to live? . . . Why isn't God taking better care of His children?" Such questions remind us that we have limited perspectives. While the Bible tells us something of God's perspective, it does not reveal all of His plans. Peter tells us that the trials that bring us grief may be used to refine our faith. Paul says that God works good out of everything and that through every experience He is seeking to make us more like Christ. James indicates that our difficulties lead to our maturity. Jesus indicated that sometimes our difficulties are designed so that people can see the work of God in our lives. (See 1 Peter 1:5–7; Romans 8:28–29; James 1:2–4; John 9:1–3.)

While all of these positive purposes are true, they still do not answer all the questions that race through our minds in the face of personal pain and loss. The call of God is that we will trust Him in the darkness as we trusted Him in the light. He has not changed, even though our circumstances have been painfully altered.

PROCESSING OUR ANGER TOWARD GOD

The problem with our anger toward God is not the anger itself but how we handle the anger. We could paraphrase Paul's words in Ephesians 4:26 by saying, "When you are angry with God, do not sin." Your anger with God is distorted anger. God has done you no wrong, but your feeling is still real anger. In fact, your anger is not a choice. Anger was your response to a situation that brought great pain to you and that you believed God could have averted. Thus, in your mind, God has treated you unfairly. Anger is the normal human response when we encounter what we perceive to be injustice. God made us with this capacity for anger. However, what we do with our anger is our responsibility. This is where we exercise the human freedom that God has given us.

The first step in responsibly handling our anger toward God is to take the anger to God. You need not be ashamed of your anger, for it is evidence of your concern for fairness. You can freely express your perception of things to God. You will not "hurt His feelings," nor will you stir up His anger. You are His child, and He wishes to share all of life with you. Your anger will not catch Him by surprise. He knows what you are experiencing and wants you to share your thoughts and feelings with Him. Biblical illustrations are abundantly clear that God does not condemn His children when they bring their anger to Him. Let's look at three examples.

The first mention of anger in the Bible is found in Genesis 4, where Cain experienced anger toward God because God accepted his brother Abel's sacrifice and did not accept his. The Scriptures say, "Cain was very angry, and his face was downcast. Then the Lord said to Cain, 'Why are you angry? Why is your face downcast? If you do what is right, will you not be accepted? But if you do not do what is right, sin is crouching at your door; it desires to have you, but you must master it'" (verses 5–7). In this first example of anger in the Scriptures, *God took the initiative* to recognize and mention Cain's anger. Apparently, Cain would have tried to hide his anger from God. In taking the initiative, God clearly indicates that He wants us to talk with Him about our anger. Anger toward God is not to be internalized. It is to be expressed to God. Interestingly, God went straight to the issue of right and wrong, which, as we have discovered, is always at the heart of our anger.

Cain encountered what he believed to be wrong behavior on the part of God. God was clearly revealing to Cain that his anger was distorted; that is, it was based on his personal perception rather than on reality. God had done Cain no wrong. Though the text does not record God's instructions, God's answer indicates that Cain knew which sacrifice was to be brought but he chose rather to disobey. Thus, God did not accept his sacrifice. God identified Cain's choice as sinful and called Cain to repentance. Sin desires to destroy us, but the challenge of God is that we must not allow this to happen. We are responsible for our own choices.

A second example is Jonah. He delivered his message of judgment: Forty days and God will destroy this city. The people of Ninevah repented; in response, God forgave them and lifted the judgment. Jonah's response to God's forgiveness was anger. He was "greatly displeased and became angry," the Scripture indicates. "He prayed to the Lord, 'O Lord, is this not what I said when I was still at home? That is why I was so quick to flee to Tarshish. I knew that you are a gracious and compassionate God, slow to anger and abounding in love, a God who relents from sending calamity. Now, O Lord, take away my life, for it is better for me to die than to live'" (Jonah 4:1–3).

Clearly, Jonah was experiencing anger, and he shared his anger with God, telling Him specifically what he believed to be unfair. God was very compassionate in His response to Jonah, as He helped Jonah examine the validity of his anger. God was helping Jonah come to understand that his preaching was not an act of futility but was indeed successful and served the purposes which God had intended.

Jonah's anger was distorted—he had been embarrassed by preaching a message of judgment when no judgment came. But repentance came, which was far more important in God's economy. We are not told what Jonah did after this conversation with God. We can only hope that he accepted God's sovereign act of forgiving the Ninevites and expressed his gratitude to God for being a part of God's redemptive work.

Elijah's anger also instructs us. In 1 Kings 18–19, we find that Elijah the prophet had confronted King Ahab with his sin and had challenged a "showdown" with the prophets of Baal. Elijah had seen the demonstration of supernatural power when fire fell from heaven and consumed the sacrifice at the praying of Elijah. The people responded, "The Lord—he is God! The Lord—he is God!" (1 Kings 18:39). The prophets of Baal were then destroyed and Elijah had experienced a great victory.

This was a great victory for God and Elijah too. The next day, however, Queen Jezebel sent word to Elijah that within twenty-four hours, she would see that he was killed. Elijah was afraid and ran for his life. The word *anger* is not used in the biblical text but its presence is evidenced in the prayer of Elijah. "'I have had enough, Lord,' he said. 'Take my life; I am no better than my ancestors'" (1 Kings 19:4).

After this desperate prayer, Elijah fell asleep. In due time, he was awakened by an angel who simply said, "'Get up and eat.' He looked around, and there by his head was a cake of bread baked over hot coals, and a jar of water." After eating, Elijah fell asleep again and was again awakened by the angel and instructed, "Get up and eat." Strengthened by the food, Elijah traveled forty days to "Horeb, the mountain of God. There he went into a cave and spent the night." (See verses 5–9.)

With Elijah fully fed and fully rested, God initiated a conversation with Elijah about his emotional state. Elijah's response was, "I have been very zealous for the Lord God Almighty. The Israelites have rejected your covenant, broken down your altars, and put your prophets to death with the sword. I am the only one left, and now they are trying to kill me too." The Lord's response was not to argue with Elijah; rather He asked Elijah to stand on the side of the mountain and observe. Elijah saw a powerful wind tear the mountains apart, an earthquake, and then a fire, but in none of these did Elijah see God. "And after the fire came a gentle whisper. When Elijah heard it, he pulled his cloak over his face and went out and stood at the mouth of the cave" (verses 10, 12–13).

Then God initiated another conversation with Elijah. Elijah repeated his prayer, expressing his disappointment that in spite of all he had done for

God, he was now the object of a manhunt. God's response would seem strange to some. He commanded Elijah to anoint a new king over Aram (Hazael), a new king over Israel (Jehu), and a prophet to succeed him (Elisha). God told Elijah that these leaders would take care of those who were opposing him. God also told Elijah that he was not the only one who worshiped God—that in fact there were seven thousand in Israel who stood true to God. Elijah accepted his new assignment from God, got up, and started on his journey. (See verses 14–18.) Elijah had processed his anger; now he was beginning to write a new chapter in his life.

All three of these biblical illustrations indicate the value of talking to God about our anger. God is our compassionate Father and wants to hear our complaints. At the same time, He is also the sovereign God who does no wrong. He will either help us understand His perspective on our present situation as He did with Cain, Jonah, and Elijah; or He may, without explanation, simply ask us to trust Him as He did with His servant Job.

Elijah illustrates *the second step in processing our anger with God: Listen to God's message.* Having expressed our honest concerns to God, we are now in a position to listen to His "quiet whisper" to us. This sometimes comes through a trusted Christian friend or through a sermon by a faithful pastor. It may come through reading a Christian book written by a believer who has walked a path similar to ours. God's word may come through the words of an old hymn or a contemporary chorus, or it may come in your personal times of reading the Scriptures. Whenever God speaks, you will know it is His voice if the message you receive is consistent with Scripture. We listen to His voice, look for the good that may come out of this painful situation, and seek to grow in Christlikeness.

In the final analysis, we must accept what has happened in our lives, choosing to believe that though we do not understand it, God will use it to accomplish His good purposes. God's own Word, the Scriptures, and His very character as a wise and sovereign God, indicate He will. Listening does not always lead to understanding, but it does lead to accepting our situation without malice toward God.

This stage of acceptance may come quickly or it may take weeks, even months. But for the believer who honestly shares his anger with God, eventually "the peace of God, which transcends all understanding," will settle upon the believer's heart and mind (Philippians 4:7).

With this peace comes the full assurance that my life is in the hands of a loving God, that what has happened does not mean He has abandoned me. Rather He is touched by the feelings of pain which I experience and interprets even my anger as an expression of my love for Him. After all, why would I be angry if I did not believe that He loved me and would look out for my interests?

After the peace of acceptance settles upon us, there is *a third stage. We report for duty* to get our next assignment from God. As long as we are alive, God is not through with us. Though Elijah wanted to die, God had kings for him to anoint. You may be diseased, discouraged, disappointed, and in deep pain, but God has plans for you, and those plans are all good. "'For I know the plans I have for you,' declares the Lord, 'plans to prosper you and not to harm you, plans to give you hope and a future'" (Jeremiah 29:11). As we get up and begin to do what God has gifted us to do, it does not mean that our pain has evaporated. It does mean that our anger has been processed and is no longer a barrier between us and God.

Edna, whom we met at the beginning of this chapter, sat in my office over fifteen years ago. Today, as she has done for many years, she is teaching a ladies' Bible study. Her classes are always crowded. "She has experienced what she teaches," one lady said. Edna freely acknowledges that her life has been greatly enriched through the loss of her only daughter. She does not seek to whitewash her pain and fully acknowledges that daily she thinks of her Jennifer and wonders what would have happened with her life if she had continued to live.

Edna has many unanswered questions, but she is willing to wait for answers. In the meantime, she has chosen to believe that God is at work even in the most painful of life's experiences.

Elijah processed his anger with God and got on with his life. Cain, on the other hand, invited his brother Abel to a secluded field and there murdered him. Cain stands forever as an example of how not to respond to anger. God held Cain accountable for his sinful behavior. Cain's life went on for many years, but it was marred by the sinful act he committed motivated by distorted anger toward God.

Every Christian who feels anger toward God will either follow the example of Cain or Elijah. If we follow Cain, we will yield to our sinful impulses and in uncontrolled anger do things that will make our lives more difficult. If we follow Elijah, we will fully share our anger with God but also listen to the "quiet whisper" which comes from God. With much or little understanding, we will choose to trust God, knowing that He too is acquainted with pain.

For the Christian who learns to process his anger toward God constructively, the future holds hope in spite of the present pain. And for many believers, history will repeat the epithet of Job. "The Lord blessed the latter part of Job's life more than the first" (Job 42:12). Like Edna and like Job, we will receive God's blessing, and He will use us in great ways.

NOTE

1. See God's extended discourses in Job 38–41. Job finally responded in trust and repented of his pride (Job 42:1–6).

WHEN YOU ARE ANGRY WITH GOD

*A*nger is the normal human response when we encounter what we perceive to be injustice. When a situation brings great pain to you and you believe God could have averted it, it is often natural to think God has treated you unfairly. Therefore you feel anger toward God. It is distorted anger (based on a *perceived* injustice), but anger nonetheless.

How do you handle this anger toward God? There are three stages to dealing responsibly with such anger.

First, take the anger to God. You can freely express your perception of things to God. You will not "hurt His feelings," nor will you stir up His anger. God is our compassionate Father and wants to hear our complaints. At the same time, He is also the sovereign God who does no wrong. He will either help us understand His perspective on our present situation or He will simply ask us to trust Him (as He did with His servant Job).

Second, listen to God's message. Once we express our honest concerns to God, we are in a position to listen to His "quiet whisper" to us. This sometimes comes through a trusted Christian friend, a pastor's sermon, or a Christian book written by a believer who has walked a path similar to ours. Other times His purpose or simply His peace will come through the words of an old hymn, a contemporary chorus, or in your personal times of reading the Scriptures. Whenever God speaks, you will know it is His voice if the message you receive is consistent with Scripture.

Third, report for further duty. As long as we are alive, God is not through with us. We will be useful tools, ready for the Master's good plans.

FOR DISCUSSION

1. Christians often experience anger toward God in the face of tragedy. We are taught that a loving God cares only for the well-being of His children. We don't understand that human tragedy often has positive spiritual purposes that God desires for His people. Recount an experience where you became angry with God over some personal tragedy or disappointment. Was your anger resolved in an effective way? How did God seem to reply to your anger at Him?

2. The book of Job is the classic Bible text dealing with obedience to God in spite of despair and tragedy. What does this text say about God and the way He answers human anger? What did you learn from Job's experience? Is there a limit to hardship that you must bear and still be faithful to the Lord?

3. Have you felt like Job at some point in your life? Why? How does God reward faithfulness during trials?

4. *Processing your anger:* You are a forty-five-year-old public speaker who also serves as an evangelist for your church. You have been a gifted speaker in the workplace and also in the service of the Lord for twenty years. After a recent visit to the doctor for what you thought was an infection, you have learned that you have an advanced case of throat cancer. The doctor's prognosis is that only surgery will save your life. The resulting surgery will mean that you will likely lose some or all of your vocal cords, and thus drastically impair your speaking ability. Since you have always attributed your gift of speech to God, you now feel betrayed by Him, that He is taking away this same gift, one that you have used in His service. Is your anger genuine or distorted? Describe how you would process your anger against God properly. What must happen in order to bring you inner peace?

Chapter 12

WHEN YOU
ARE ANGRY
AT YOURSELF

*W*hite fluffy clouds are floating beneath the blue sky this Saturday morning. The radio announces it is 65 degrees at 8 A.M., and Seth decides this is a perfect day to repair the steps leading to the deck behind his house. Within fifteen minutes, Seth is outside, hammer in hand. A minute later Seth hits his thumb with the hammer.

The intense physical pain is matched by his intense anger at himself. The thoughts jump wildly in his mind: *How stupid! Why did I keep my fingers on that nail? I should have hired a carpenter to do this. I know I'm not good at this stuff.* He looks at his swelling thumb. He can not bend it without sharp, stabbing pain. *Now I've got to go to the emergency room; I've lost the whole day. I know I've fractured the bone in my thumb. I can't believe I did this!*

What is Seth experiencing on this beautiful morning? Anger directed at himself. He believes that the pain in his thumb, which is now running up his arm, is because of his own careless behavior. His anger grows as he concludes that he made a wrong decision when he chose to repair the steps himself. Anger piles upon anger when he realizes that his careless act has cost him the rest of the day in the emergency room. *I was careless. I was foolish. I was wrong.* These are the messages that accompany Seth's anger.

From time to time, most people feel anger toward themselves. Usually it is because we perceive that we have done something wrong: We have acted carelessly, foolishly, or irresponsibly. In the heat of this anger, our thoughts are self-condemning. The emotions of guilt and, sometimes, shame accompany our anger.

As we have noted throughout this book, anger is an emotional and physical response of intense displeasure when we encounter someone or something which we perceive to be wrong, unfair, or unjust. When we experience anger toward ourselves, it is because we perceive that we are the ones guilty of the wrongdoing, the unkindness, the injustice, or, as in the case of Seth, the careless act. This anger toward self may be mild, medium, or malicious depending on what one has done. If I get to my car parked in the garage and realize that I left my key in the second-story bedroom, my anger toward self may be mild. If I lock my keys in the car in the shopping center parking lot, my anger may be medium. But if I lose my keys on a hunting trip one hundred miles from the nearest civilization, my anger at myself may be malicious.

SOURCES OF PERSONAL ANGER

The events that stimulate this self-focused anger may surface in any area of one's life. *When we don't live up to our expectations,* that is, we fail to accomplish what we know we are capable of doing in our vocation, hobbies, relationships, or church life, we may experience anger at ourselves.

Jon was a young business executive, a hard worker and rising star in the company. But on Tuesday night, his wife, Bev, found him moping in self-condemnation. "I can't believe I left one of the most important elements out of my report. When my colleague mentioned it, it was so obvious. I can't believe I overlooked that. It makes me look so stupid and to think the VP was there. He never comes to those meetings. I just can't believe it."

Jenna usually comes home from choir rehearsal in a positive, excited mood, but tonight Mac notices that she is quiet and withdrawn. "How did choir rehearsal go?" he asked. "It was awful," she said. "I don't know why I tried out for that solo. I should never have auditioned. I sounded terrible. I know I can do better than that. I don't know what happened. My voice just tightened up. I sounded like a screeching owl."

When Brad comes home from playing golf, he is usually feeling relaxed and "on top of the world." But Thursday evening when Jennifer asked him, "How did your game go?" he said, "I don't even want to talk about it. I think it's the worst game I have ever played. I don't know what was wrong with me. I didn't do anything right."

Jon, Jenna, and Brad are all experiencing anger toward themselves because they did not live up to what they know they are capable of doing. They reason that "not to do one's best is inexcusable." Therefore, they are angry with themselves for their poor performance.

Most of us sometimes act carelessly or foolishly. When these acts result in detrimental consequences, *we tend to get angry with ourselves for being foolish or careless.* Bruce was driving down a straight stretch of interstate highway in his newly leased car. He was trying to find the buttons to activate his CD player when he ran into the back of a slow moving pickup truck. He was furious with himself. *I can't believe I did that! I've always lectured Andy to never mess with the radio when you're driving. Keep your eyes on the road. I've told him that a hundred times and now I do something stupid like this!*

Marilyn was in a hurry when she stepped on the stool to reach the bowl on the top shelf. The stool slid and the next thing she knew, she was on the floor with broken glass all around her. Marilyn's first thought was, *Why did I have to be in such a hurry? I knew that stool was unstable. If I'd taken more time, this would not have happened.* Moments later when she realized that her arm was broken, she was even more angry at herself. *Now I've messed up the whole weekend,* she thought. *I've got to go to the doctor instead of taking Ginny to see her grandmother. I have got to slow down. I feel like I'm on a treadmill.* Then she realized what she had just thought and told herself, *Well, I guess I will slow down with this broken arm.* Careless, thoughtless actions often create situations that stimulate self-focused anger.

Perhaps the area that brings *the most intense anger to the Christian is when we violate our own strongly held values.* The Christian husband who is sexually unfaithful to his wife may try to blame her for his indiscretions but may later experience intense personal anger for allowing himself to fall into immorality.

Ken is a committed Christian who found himself lying and later "getting caught." He experienced anger toward himself. *Why did I do that? I didn't even have to lie. It didn't make any real difference. I don't know why I did that. I am so upset with myself.* These are the kinds of thoughts that accompanied Ken's anger. Any violation of one's moral values has the potential for eventually stimulating self-focused anger. The anger may come when the individual first realizes what he has done, or it may come when the wrongdoing is discovered by others and made public. As the individual begins to suffer the consequences of wrongdoing, his self-focused anger may arise.

Such anger is often accompanied by feelings of guilt. Anger and guilt should lead to repentance and refreshing forgiveness, which we will discuss later. However, sometimes we wallow in our guilt and turn our anger inward.

UNHEALTHY RESPONSES

Whatever the source of the anger we feel toward ourselves, we must learn to process it constructively. Two negative ways of expressing our anger are explosion and implosion, both of which we discussed in chapter 6. These same destructive methods may be used in responding to the anger we feel toward ourselves. If we explode, then we give ourselves angry words and may treat ourselves with physical abuse. Our verbal explosions may be in private or in the presence of family members, but we berate ourselves verbally. "I can't believe I can be so stupid. I don't ever do anything right. How did I do this? I am so ashamed of myself. I don't think I can ever face the world again. I wish I could just die." Such verbal tirades may sometimes be accompanied by physical acts of violence. Pulling one's hair, scratching oneself, beating one's head against the wall or floor, cutting one's body with sharp instruments, and suicide attempts are all destructive ways of responding to anger toward oneself.

Implosion means that while we are not audibly expressing negative messages toward ourselves nor inflicting physical harm, we are attacking ourselves mentally and silently. On the outside we may appear to be calm but inside we are raging against ourselves. *I deserve to suffer; look what I did. I was so stupid. I don't know why anybody would believe in me again. I did what I knew was wrong. I don't deserve forgiveness.* Sometimes the thoughts are highly condemning. *My life is useless. I don't deserve to be happy. I don't have any reason to go on living.* These are the emotional mental records that play in the minds of those who internalize anger toward themselves. Such internal self-condemnation often has a detrimental effect upon the body and brings on physical problems usually associated with the digestive and neurological systems of the body.

Obviously, neither explosion nor implosion are satisfactory ways to respond to one's anger toward self. How then must the Christian respond to this self-focused anger?

PROPER RESPONSES TO PERSONAL ANGER

Let me suggest a positive approach to processing anger toward oneself. The following five steps represent healthy responses to your anger.

First, admit your anger. Admit it to yourself, to a trusted friend or family member, to a counselor or pastor, but admit that you are experiencing anger toward yourself. "I am really feeling angry at myself" is the first statement of healing. Admit the other thoughts and feelings that accompany your anger. Perhaps: "I feel so disappointed in myself. I feel so foolish or stupid for letting this happen. I feel like I have let people down, including myself and God. I feel so irresponsible." Express as clearly as you can what you are thinking and feeling.

If you like, write the statements down. Say them aloud to yourself and say them in prayer to God. But admit and declare your anger.

Second, examine your anger. Anger toward oneself may either be definitive anger or distorted anger, as discussed in chapter 4. Definitive anger at myself means that my anger grows out of an actual wrong which I have committed. Distorted anger means that my anger has arisen from a perceived wrong rather than a real wrong. Both must be processed, but it is helpful to know the kind of anger that you are dealing with. There is a vast difference between the anger Seth felt when he hit his thumb with a hammer and the anger a husband feels who has been sexually unfaithful to his wife. The latter is an immoral act, and the anger is definitive. On the other hand, hitting one's thumb with a hammer is not immoral. Seth committed no immoral act. Seth must examine his perceptions.

Seth initially perceives that holding a nail with his fingers was a careless act. He concludes that with his level of carpentry skills, he should not have attempted to repair the stairs but should have hired a professional carpenter. Are these perceptions true? Maybe yes; maybe no. Only Seth can ultimately answer these questions. Was the nail already firmly implanted in the wood? If so, his fingers were unneeded and thus it was a careless act. If needed, he could have held the nail in place with pliers, although not even a beginning carpenter would do this. Holding a nail in place with a thumb and forefinger is a perfectly normal operation if one is about to drive a nail. Did he allow his attention to be diverted when the hammer was coming toward the nail? If so, perhaps that was a careless act. Unless Seth is an absolute klutz in working with his hands, he probably had the ability to repair the stairs and thus did not need to hire a carpenter.

Seth may conclude that he actually was careless. If so, then he confesses his carelessness to God, accepts forgiveness, and seeks to learn from the experience. Seth might pray, "Father, forgive me for being careless with the body You have given me. Thank You for Your love and Your forgiveness. Help me to learn from this painful experience. I love You and pray for the healing of my thumb." After such a prayer, Seth's anger subsides while his thumb continues to throb. He has handled his anger in a constructive way.

Perhaps instead Seth concludes that indeed he was not careless, that hitting his thumb was simply an accident; hammers and nail heads do not always attract each other, and the eye and the hand are not always coordinated. Seth realizes that what he experienced is common to any person who has ever picked up a hammer. His painful experience was a result of being human and living in a fallen world filled with briars, snakes, and hammers that have a mind of their own. In that case, his prayer might be: "Father, thank You for letting me be a part of the human race. My thumb is still throbbing, but I thank You that it's still there. Help me not to give up on repairing the stairs simply because I hurt myself. Help my thumb to heal and give me wisdom on how to use the rest of this day." In this case, Seth's anger was distorted anger. He really wasn't careless. His anger toward himself needs to be released and he needs to affirm his worth as a child of God who is imperfect and living in an imperfect world.

The husband who has been unfaithful to his wife has a much bigger issue with which to deal. He has broken one of God's clearly stated moral laws. He is feeling angry with himself, and his anger is definitive, rising from a moral wrong. With his anger he may feel guilt, shame, and embarrassment. All of these are normal and expected feelings when one has violated moral principles. He feels guilty because he is guilty; he feels shame because he did a shameful thing; he is embarrassed because others know about his sinful act. His anger at himself is real and must be processed, which brings us to the third step.

Third, confess wrongdoing to God and accept His forgiveness. There is only one appropriate way to process anger toward oneself which arises from one's own sin. That way was prescribed by the apostle John: "If we confess our sins, he is faithful and just and will forgive us our sins and purify us from all unrighteousness" (1 John 1:9). This is the clear message of all Scripture. God loves us and wants to have fellowship with us, but because He is holy, our sin breaks that fellowship, and He must treat us as disobedient children. This means that He will rebuke and discipline us. (See Hebrews 12:5–11.) But when we are willing to confess our sins, He is fully willing to forgive our sins. That is what the cross of Christ is all about. He took the punishment for our sins so that God could forgive us and still be just. Our part is to admit that we need His forgiveness. When we reach out for His forgiveness, He always responds in forgiving love and makes us pure again. Once again, we can now enjoy His fellowship.

When our sin has been not only against ourselves and God but against another person, then we are to confess our wrongdoing to the person we sinned against and request his forgiveness. The apostle Paul practiced this in his own life. "So I strive always to keep my conscience clear [empty] before God and man" (Acts 24:16). We empty our conscience of guilt toward God by confessing to God, and we empty our conscience toward man by confessing to the person we sinned against. True repentance of sin is always accompanied by a desire to admit our wrongdoing and to make restitution to those against whom we have sinned. Confession is the first step in restitution.

Zacchaeus, the dishonest tax collector, demonstrated this principle when he encountered Jesus. Zacchaeus said, "'Look, Lord! Here and now I give half of my possessions to the poor, and if I have cheated anybody out of anything, I will pay back four times the amount.' Jesus said to him, 'Today salvation has come to this house'" (Luke 19:8–9). Jesus did not forgive Zacchaeus because Zacchaeus offered to make restitution; his restitution was evidence that he acknowledged Jesus as Lord. When one is right with God, his desire is also to be right with man. The husband who repents of an adulterous relationship and confesses to God will experience God's forgiveness. He can never experience his wife's forgiveness until he has acknowledged his wrong. If she chooses to forgive him, he then has the opportunity to work at rebuilding his wife's trust and bringing new life to the marriage.

Having experienced God's forgiveness and perhaps the forgiveness of the person we sinned against, we are now ready for step four.

Fourth, choose to forgive yourself. Forgiving oneself is much like forgiving someone who has sinned against you. Forgiving someone else means that you choose to no longer hold the sin against them. You will accept them back into your life as though they had not sinned, and you will seek to continue building your relationship with them. Their sin is no longer a barrier in your relationship. If the wall is seen as a symbol of their sins against you, forgiveness tears down the wall. Forgiveness allows the two of you to communicate again, to listen to each other with a view to understanding. It opens up the potential of working together as a team.

As noted in chapter 8, forgiveness does not necessarily remove the hurt, the pain, or the memory of wrongdoing. But it does not allow these to hinder the relationship. With time, these will heal. Nor does forgiveness remove all of the results of sin. For example, trust is often destroyed when someone sins against us. Forgiveness does not automatically restore trust. Trust must be built by the repentant person being trustworthy in the future. If he remains trustworthy in the weeks and months after repentance and confession, trust will grow strong again.

These same principles are true in forgiving oneself. At its root, self-forgiveness is a choice. We feel pained at our wrongdoing. We wish we had never sinned. The reality is that we have. But we have also confessed our sin to God and received His forgiveness. If our sin was against others, we have confessed it and requested forgiveness, and we are seeking to rebuild that relationship. Now it is time to forgive ourselves. We must choose to do so. No positive purpose is served by berating ourselves explosively or implosively. All such behavior is destructive and thus a sinful response to our anger. This too needs to be confessed to God.

Choosing to forgive ourselves is best done in the context of prayer, letting God witness our self-forgiveness. The following prayer may help you express your thoughts and feelings to God.

Father, You know the wrong I committed. I have already confessed it to You, and I know that You have forgiven it. In fact, Your Word says that You no longer remember that against me. I thank You for Your forgiveness. You also know that over the past few weeks I have put myself down, beaten myself with destructive words, told myself that I am not worthy of living, that I deserve to be punished forever, that I wish I could die. I know that these self-destructive thoughts are not pleasing to You. Because You have given me life and because I have trusted in Jesus, I am Your child. I have no right to condemn myself after You have forgiven me. I confess these wrong attitudes to You, and I ask for Your forgiveness.

I thank You that You love me and that You freely forgive. Now understanding who I am—Your child—I forgive myself for the wrongs I have done. Even though the pain may follow me for a long time and when I think of my failures I may weep, I will no longer allow my past failures to keep me from doing the positive things You have called me to do.

With Your help, I remove those failures from my life forever and I commit myself to following You in the future.

Such a prayer, offered sincerely, can be the decisive step in forgiving oneself. As in forgiving others, this self-forgiveness does not remove all the pain or memories of your past failure, nor does it necessarily remove all the results of your failure. For example, if one's sin was lying or stealing, one may still have to face the results of those actions. Accepting God's forgiveness and forgiving oneself does not keep the thief out of jail. What forgiveness does is to release you from the bondage of your past failures and give you the freedom to make the most of the future. That brings us to step five.

Fifth, focus on positive actions. You are now in a position to change the course of your life. You can learn from your failures. Sometimes people make the mistake of trying never to think again about the failure. Their reasoning is, *Now that God has forgiven me and I've forgiven myself, I don't want to think about it anymore.* This, I believe, is a mistake. The fact is, we can learn much from our failures. The Scriptures indicate that God wants to work good out of everything that happens to us. (See Romans 8:28.) My part is to cooperate with Him. "Father, help me to learn the lessons I need to learn from my past failures" is a prayer that God welcomes.

What are the factors that led you to yield to temptation in the past? Those are things that need to be changed. For example, if you fell to the temptation of alcohol or drug abuse, it may be because you put yourself in a situation that fostered drinking or drug use. In the future, you must not allow this to happen. If your failure was sexual immorality, then you must remove yourself from the environment which would encourage you to repeat that failure. If your sin was fostered by not having a daily devotional time with God, then this needs to be built into your daily schedule. "What caused me to fail in the past?" and "What changes do I need to make to prevent this in the future?" are thoughtful questions that can lead to constructive growth.

In addition to learning from past failures, you are now in a position to take positive steps to make your future brighter. This may involve reading books, attending seminars, talking with friends, or counseling with a Christian counselor or pastor. These are the kind of steps that give you new information and insights with which to direct your future. If your sin was against a family member or friend, this is the time to focus on positive action toward that person. I do not mean that you seek to manipulate the individual into forgiving you or thinking more positively of you. Manipulation is an effort to control another person. This is never constructive in human relationships. I am talking rather of acts of love that reach out to do something good to the other person without expecting anything in return. Unconditional love is not payment for services rendered nor is it a bribe to get what we want. It is a true effort to enhance someone else's life simply because we care about them. It is what God does for us every day.

THE POWER OF LOVE

When it comes to positive action, love is the greatest. The Scriptures indicate that if we choose to live a life of unconditional love for other people, God will "[pour] out his love into our hearts by the Holy Spirit" (Romans 5:5). Loving is God's lifestyle. It is central in God's desire for us. "A new command I give you: Love one another. As I have loved you, so you must love one another," Jesus said. "By this all men will know that you are my disciples, if you love one another" (John 13:34–35).

Love is to be the distinguishing mark of the Christian. As you take positive action in loving the person you have wronged, you cannot force him to reciprocate your love, but you can be confident that love is the most influential weapon for good in the world. If your love is truly unconditional and is expressed in actions as well as words, you are doing the most powerful thing you can do for another person. However the individual responds, you will feel good about yourself because you are following the teachings of Jesus. You have been forgiven by God, perhaps by others, and you have forgiven yourself and are facing the future with hope.

WHEN YOU ARE ANGRY AT YOURSELF

*W*hether the source of personal anger is an actual or a perceived wrongdoing, we must learn to process personal anger constructively. Neither explosive or implosive responses are constructive. Here are five healthy steps in dealing with anger toward yourself.

First, admit your anger. Admit it to yourself and even to someone else. If you like, write the statements down. Say them aloud to yourself and say them in prayer to God.

Second, examine your anger. Determine whether the anger is definitive or distorted. Definitive anger is based on real wrongdoing that must be dealt with, whereas distorted anger may be causing illegitimate guilt, shame, and embarrassment.

Third, confess wrongdoing to God and accept His forgiveness. When anger toward oneself arises from one's own sin, the appropriate response is confession to God and acceptance of His forgiveness. (See 1 John 1:9.) If our wrongdoing has hurt someone else, we should confess our wrong to them and ask their forgiveness.

Fourth, choose to forgive yourself. We feel pained at our wrongdoing. But once we have confessed our sin to God and received His forgiveness, we must forgive ourselves. No positive purpose is served by berating ourselves explosively or implosively. All such behavior is destructive and thus a sinful response to our anger. This too needs to be confessed to God. In prayer, we let God witness our self-forgiveness.

Fifth, focus on positive actions. Learn from your failures; take positive steps to strengthen the likelihood the wrongdoing will not recur.

FOR DISCUSSION

1. Besides venting our anger at others, including God, we often focus our anger inwardly toward ourselves. We do this when we do something "dumb" or forget an important element that we should have remembered or known. Often the anger is minimized, but it can sometimes lead to explosive or implosive behavior reflected toward ourselves. Share with members of your group an experience of self-anger. Was the effect of the anger minor or major? Did it result in a modest mental hand slap or did it result in some more serious impact? Were there any long-lasting or serious results from the anger? Was anyone else affected by the anger? How?

2. Review the five steps we can use in handling self-directed anger, summarized on the previous page. This chapter reminds us of the principles of admitting and examining anger covered in previous chapters, as well as confession and forgiveness by the one committing the wrong. Now you are asked to forgive yourself. How do you forgive yourself? Can others help in this process? What makes forgiveness of oneself seem real?

3. Step five asks us to focus on positive action. What positive action do you take if you have forgotten to get a birthday present for your mother? Dropped and broken a valuable sculpture? Created a financial burden at your work through careless oversight? Discuss ideas among the group.

4. *Processing your anger:* You are a college history professor. You just finished giving a final examination for your senior-level American history seminar. Inadvertently, you misplace the folder with the exams. You know that several of your brightest students are counting on top grades to get them into prestigious graduate schools, while others are just hoping to pass. No opportunity for retesting exists. What feelings of self-anger are you experiencing? How will you process these feelings to reach a satisfactory resolution for you and your students?

Chapter 13

WHEN YOU ENCOUNTER AN ANGRY PERSON

*S*itting in my office one April afternoon counseling a young couple, I heard a loud rapping on my office door. "Pardon me," I said to the couple, and I stood and walked to the door. As I stepped outside, I saw a man who appeared to be in his early fifties. He wasted no time in stating his mission.

"I'll tell you right now, the church will pay for my muffler. Those speed bumps are too high," he said, pointing to the church's parking lot adjacent to my office. "They pulled the muffler right off my car and I wasn't going fast. They should never have installed those speed bumps. If they tore my muffler off, they'll tear somebody else's muffler off. The church is responsible and they are going to pay for it."

He said all of this without taking a breath and in his loudest staccato voice. His face was red. His eyes were glaring, and his nostrils were flared. I knew I was in the presence of an angry man.

I closed the door to my office. (Up until this time, my hand was still on the knob and the door still ajar. Perhaps subconsciously, I was planning my way of escape in case he got violent.) I said to him softly, "Now tell me again exactly what happened to your car." Again his angry words began to flow.

"I was driving through the parking lot and when I went over that speed bump, it pulled my muffler right off the car. I don't know when they put those speed bumps in. They are too high and somebody is going to pay for my muffler."

"Now tell me exactly which direction were you traveling and which speed bump did you hit?" I continued.

SLOWING DOWN

His voice lowered a bit and his pace slowed as he said, "I was coming from the activities building around toward Peace Haven Road. It's the speed bump at the end of this building. Why did they put a speed bump there? It's too close to the street."

"And did it pull your muffler completely off your car?" I asked. "No, it's still hanging on at the back, but it's dragging on the street. I've got to find some wire to attach it so I can drive home. It's not right. The church should pay for my muffler."

Feeling that I had heard his story and understood the situation, I said to him, "I can see why you would be upset. I would be upset if that had happened to me. I didn't realize the speed bumps were that high, but if it pulled your muffler off, it will likely pull someone else's muffler off and we need to have it fixed. I can assure you that the church will pay for having your muffler repaired. That's the least we can do. If you will send me the bill, I'll make sure that you get reimbursed. If I weren't counseling with a couple, I would go down and try to help you attach your muffler. But I think you will find one of our maintenance men on the first floor. Perhaps he could help you find some wire. I really appreciate your sharing this with me because if you hadn't taken the time to come up here, I would not know that there is a problem with the speed bump. And obviously we need to have it fixed. I appreciate your taking the time and effort to come up and share that with me."

Now with a calm voice, he said, "Well, I just felt like you'd like to know it. Did you say that you're counseling a couple?"

"Yes," I said.

"Oh, I'm so sorry I interrupted you," he said, "and I'm sorry I beat on your door. I should not have been so upset."

"I understand. It was a pretty loud rap," I said smiling.

He smiled and said, "I know. I'm ashamed of myself. I shouldn't have gotten so out of control." Not wanting to add to his guilt, I said, "All of us sometimes get out of control. It's good when we realize it and are willing to admit it. I've been there. I know, but I genuinely appreciate your sharing the information with me about the speed bump. And we will have it corrected."

Backing away from me and moving toward the door of my outer office, he said, "Thank you, and again, I'm sorry I disturbed you." As he opened the door and walked into the hallway, I said, "It's OK. Thank you."

I had never seen the man before nor since. But I have often used this experience as an example of how to respond to an angry person. Perhaps I use it because this is one time when I feel I did it right. (Incidentally, I never received the man's repair bill for the muffler. I can only assume he was too ashamed of his behavior to divulge his name and address.) The speed bumps had been installed two weeks before. As far as I know, his was the only muffler that was ever attacked, although we did have some complaints that the speed bumps were too high. The next week, we had them shaved.

THE PROPER RESPONSES TO ANGRY PEOPLE

From time to time most of us encounter angry people. Some are out of control. Others are trying hard not to be verbally or physically abusive, but inside they are steaming over what they consider to be an injustice. It may be a neighbor who believes that you have treated him unfairly. It may be a fellow employee who perceives that what you have done is wrong. It may be a fellow student who accuses you of cheating or is angry with you because you will not cheat. It may be a mother-in-law or a brother-in-law, a father or a son, an uncle or a nephew, or it may be someone you have never seen before such as the man with the wounded muffler. How are we to respond to these angry people?

Let me suggest seven steps. The first three are extremely important. *First, listen. Second, listen. Third, listen.* The best thing you can do for an angry person is to listen to his story. Having heard it, ask him to repeat it. Having heard it a second time, ask additional questions to clarify the situation. Listen at least three times before you give a response. That's why I call listening the first three steps in responding to angry people.

In the first round of listening, you become aware you are in the presence of an angry person, and you get something of the person's story and the heart of why she is angry. In the second round of listening, she begins to see that you are taking her seriously, that you really want to understand what happened, and you are not condemning her anger. In the third round, she is scraping up the details and making sure you get the whole story; at this point, the individual usually begins to calm down, as she senses that you are trying to understand her. It takes at least three rounds of listening, sometimes four, for the angry person to get out all of his or her concerns.

If you respond to someone's anger before you have thoroughly heard their story, you will not defuse the anger. You will compound it. Inside the mind of the angry person is a deep sense that he has been wronged. He is expressing his anger to you either because you are involved or he thinks you have the power to help. When you listen to him, you are respecting his right to be angry, you are treating him as you wish someone would treat you if you were angry. You are listening in a sympathetic manner, trying to understand the person's thoughts and feelings. This is what all of us want when we are angry. Why not give it to the angry people whom you encounter? Listening paves the pathway to understanding, which brings us to our fourth step.

Next, seek to understand the angry person's plight. Put yourself in her shoes and try to view the world through her eyes. Try to understand what stimulated her anger. Ask yourself, "Would I be angry in the same situation?" Try to identify with the person by visualizing yourself having experienced what that person has experienced.

It was not hard for me to identify with the angry man whose muffler lay beneath his car in the church parking lot. Had it been my car, I would likely have felt similar angry feelings. I may not have responded the way he responded, but it was not difficult to understand his anger.

It is true that sometimes the person's anger may be distorted. He may not have all the facts. He may be overlooking his own responsibility. My angry intruder may have been speeding through the parking lot. After all, that's why the speed bumps had been installed. They had been in place for two weeks, and his was the first muffler to be abducted. On the other hand, perhaps his muffler was hanging lower than the mufflers on other cars. These were details of which I had no knowledge and which were of little concern to him. It would have been useless for me to have raised those issues; they would simply have been attempts to defend the church and to point blame toward him. Both of these would likely have escalated the anger rather than helped to process it.

If you can listen long enough to get all the thoughts that are rumbling through the mind of the angry person, you will likely be able to understand why he is angry. Whether one's interpretation of the situation is correct is not the issue at this point. What you are trying to do is to understand what the person is seeing in the situation. Given his interpretation, can you see how he would feel angry? This is not the stage in which to argue with the person about his interpretation. What you are trying to do is to understand his anger so that you might help him process it.

Marsha and Suzanne worked on the same assembly line. Marsha heard by way of the grapevine that Suzanne had told their supervisor that Marsha would be happy to work on New Year's Day because she hated football games and would like to have a reason to get out of the house. Marsha had been chewing on this tidbit of information for the last two hours. As she did her work, she was thinking, *I really wouldn't mind working that day, but Suzanne had no right to tell the supervisor that. She's simply looking out for her own interests and taking advantage of me.* Her anger was beginning to brew. Two hours later when the holiday work schedule was posted and Marsha saw her own name on January 1, she exploded.

She went straight to Suzanne and said, "You had no right to tell the supervisor that I would be happy to work on a holiday. You had not asked me about that. Don't ever speak for me. You are always looking out for your own interests and you are taking advantage of me. Don't think you can control my life. I don't appreciate what you did."

Suzanne is blown away by Marsha's flow of words. She has no idea what Marsha is talking about. So she says calmly, "Marsha, sit down and tell me exactly what you are talking about."

"You know what I'm talking about," Marsha continued. "You told the supervisor that I would be happy to work on January 1 because I hate football games and I would like an opportunity to get out of the house. Well, that's partially true, but you had no right to set me up to work on a holiday. That's wrong and you know that's wrong. And that's why I'm upset."

Suzanne moved to round three. "Are you saying that you think that I told the supervisor that you wanted to work on New Year's Day and that she should assign you that holiday rather than me?" Suzanne asked.

"That's exactly what I'm saying," Marsha said, "and you know that's not right."

"Then I can see why you would be so angry," Suzanne said. "It makes sense. If I thought that you had done the same thing to me, I would be upset also. I don't blame you for being angry. I would probably be angrier than you are if I thought you had done that to me. But let me tell you what really happened. The supervisor came to me and asked if I would like to work on January 1. I told her that I preferred not to, but I would be happy to if she couldn't get anyone else. I did say, 'You may want to check with Marsha. I know that she's not particularly fond of staying at home on New Year's Day. She might be interested in working.'

"I thought the supervisor would go to you and ask if you wanted to work. I was certainly not telling her to assign you to work without asking you. I knew how you felt about the football games on a holiday, and I was simply suggesting that she talk with you about it. But if the supervisor didn't talk with you about it, I can certainly see how you would have gotten upset. I would have gotten upset also.

"I'm still willing to work on the first if you prefer," Suzanne continued. "In fact, I think you worked last year. It's probably my turn and if you don't want to work, I certainly would be open to doing so."

Marsha was now calm, and Suzanne and she talked further about what had happened. And the whole matter was resolved. Marsha agreed that she really preferred to work on the first; she just didn't like the idea of being manipulated. Now that she realized that was not the case, everything was fine.

Suzanne demonstrated the next step in the process of responding to an angry person. After her three rounds of listening, she understood why Marsha was angry. Then she *expressed her understanding to Marsha* when she said, "If I thought you had done that to me, I would also be angry." She did not jump in and set Marsha straight on the facts; that would come later. Rather, she expressed understanding of Marsha's anger by putting herself in Marsha's situation. Suzanne knew that she had done Marsha no wrong, but she also understood that in Marsha's mind she was guilty. By trying to put ourselves in another person's shoes and understand the situation as she sees it, it is not difficult to understand why the person would be angry. Once we understand, we express understanding. Suzanne demonstrated an excellent way to express understanding when she said: "If I were in your shoes and saw the situation as you see it, I would also be angry." This puts the angry person at ease. It says to them that they are not weird for feeling angry; that if you were in their situation you would also feel angry. You have now removed the adversarial nature of the conversation. You are no longer their adversary; you are standing beside them in their anger. You are acknowledging not only that you understand their anger but that you too would be angry in a similar situation.

Having expressed understanding of the other person's anger, you are now ready for *step six: share additional information that may shed light on the subject.* In the case of Suzanne, this meant telling Marsha exactly what happened in her conversation with the supervisor. It was the sharing of this information that allowed Marsha the freedom to let her anger subside and to realize that Suzanne had not wronged her. If anyone had wronged her, it was the supervisor by not checking with her before making the work assignment. But since Marsha had actually wanted to work on the holiday, any anger she felt toward the supervisor was short-lived.

Often the person we encounter has distorted anger; she does not have all of the facts or she is misinterpreting the facts. We do the person a great service when we share our perception of what happened. But if this is shared too early in the process, we will not be heard and we will find ourselves in a heated argument with the angry person. For example, what if after Marsha's initial explosion, Suzanne had said the following: "Let me tell you one thing, Marsha. Don't come over here exploding on me. I did not say that to the supervisor. I don't know who told you that, but they were wrong. Now you get out of my work space and don't come back over here talking to me like that again"? Such a response could have set into motion animosity between Marsha and Suzanne that could have lasted for years. The tragedy is that such responses are all too common.

"Setting the person straight" immediately after she has unleashed her first statement of anger is a serious mistake. It will almost always engender argument and seldom leads to a positive resolution. Friendships are often destroyed by such angry counterattacks.

It is important to share the facts as you see them but only after you have listened, understood, and expressed understanding for the other person's anger. Then your information will likely be received and processed in a positive way by the angry person. This leads to resolution of the issues and restoration of the friendship.

The final step in responding to the angry person is confession and restitution. If you realize that the angry person's anger is definitive; that is, you have genuinely wronged her—intentionally or unintentionally, what you did or said was unfair and hurt her deeply—then it is time for your confession and efforts to make right the wrong you have committed. If Suzanne had done what Marsha thought she had done, namely manipulated the supervisor in order to get herself out of working on a holiday, then it would have called for honest confession.

What would such a confession sound like? It would include accepting responsibility and asking for forgiveness. For instance, Suzanne might have said, "Marsha, you're right. I realized after I did it that it was wrong. I should not have done that even though I knew that you didn't like the football games on New Year's Day; I should not have used that information to try to get you assigned to a holiday work schedule. I was thinking about how much I wanted to be with my grandchildren on that day, and I went overboard in trying to make that happen. I realize that I was wrong and I'm sorry. I will go to the supervisor and request that she change the schedule and let me work on the first if you prefer. If you don't want to work on that day, it's only fair that I should work. What I did was wrong, and I'm sincerely sorry. I hope that you will be able to forgive me." Such a sincere confession and offer to make restitution will likely clear the air and resolve the issue between Marsha and Suzanne.

To try to defend one's own actions when they have in fact been wrong is an effort in futility and will again lead to argument and seldom to resolution. Many of us find it very difficult to admit that we have done or said something wrong. To admit failure diminishes our self-esteem, and thus we fight to be right even when we know we are wrong. Such behavior ultimately is to the detriment of one's self-esteem. When we know that what we've done is wrong and we defend ourselves rather than admitting our wrong, we may be able to convince others by our defense, but we do not convince ourselves. Our conscience begins to fill with guilt and we feel badly about ourselves.

Defending our own wrongdoing is never a road to mental or relational health. On the other hand, confession and restitution almost always lead not only to emotional health but to strong, healthy relationships.

I believe that these seven steps (summarized on page 178 in "From One Side to Another") are the most productive way to respond to an angry person. Let me urge you not to rush through steps one, two, and three. Listening, listening, and listening again is the foundation for gaining understanding so that in turn you can express understanding. In addition, recognize that steps one through five are crucial for creating an atmosphere where you can then share the facts as you see them and thus resolve the issue; or, if wrongdoing has been committed, lead to confession and restitution that can bring resolution. The other person's anger subsides because you have helped him thoroughly process his anger. And in so doing, you have maintained a positive relationship with the other person.

WRONG RESPONSE ONE: TRYING TO CAP THE ANGER

A word of caution against two common negative approaches in trying to respond to an angry person. They both are common, and they both are negative. The first is trying to put a cap on the other person's anger. Parents are often guilty of this. "If you can't talk to me without yelling, then shut up and go to your room." Such a statement made by a parent to a child stops the flow of the child's emotions and bottles them within the child. Take two swallows from a Pepsi, screw the cap back on the plastic bottle, and shake it vigorously and you will have a visual picture of what is happening inside the child whose parent made this statement. The child is in his room, the door is closed, the cap is on his anger, but inside the carbonated feelings are emerging. When the cap does come off, you will have a child in rage. If the cap never comes off, you will have a child in depression or one who exhibits passive-aggressive behavior. That is, his anger will never be expressed directly but indirectly. By his behavior, he will do things "to get back" at the parent.

Seeking to put a cap on another person's anger is perhaps the worst way to respond to an angry person. The only positive response to such action is that the parent gets momentary calm, but that is a high price to pay for such temporary and shallow peace. We may not like the way the angry person is speaking to us, but the fact that he is sharing his anger is positive. The anger cannot be processed positively if it is held inside. It needs to be expressed, even if it is expressed with a loud voice.

In order to help the angry person, you must temporarily overlook the loudness of his voice, the glare of her eyes, and the intensity of the body language. You must look beyond all of this to the heart of the matter: What is the person angry about? What wrong does he perceive has been committed? It is dealing with this wrong that is the issue. Whether the wrong is definitive or distorted, it is real in the mind of the angry person. If we do not listen to the person's message, the anger will not be processed positively but will later show up in outrageous behavior, depression, or, tragically for some, suicide. Attempting to put a cap on another person's anger is an effort in futility.

WRONG RESPONSE TWO:
MIRRORING THE BEHAVIOR

A second negative way to respond to the angry person is to mirror his behavior. By this, I mean that you allow his out-of-control, angry behavior to stimulate the same kind of behavior in yourself. She is yelling at you, so you yell at her. He is throwing Coke bottles at you, so you throw a brick at him. Such a response to an angry person obviously expands the problem. One angry person who is out of control is enough. We don't need two angry people out of control.

Thus, when you encounter an angry person, it is time to pray, "Oh, Father, please help me to be redemptive in this situation. Give me a listening ear. Let me get beyond the angry behavior so that I can understand why this person is angry and try to help them resolve it." Such a prayer is in keeping with the admonition of James, who said, "Everyone should be quick to listen, slow to speak and slow to become angry, for man's anger does not bring about the righteous life that God desires" (James 1:19–20).

An angry person who is out of control needs someone to help him process the anger. He does not need someone who will fight with him but someone who will wade through the fog to get to the root of the angry person's behavior. A fire will burn out faster if you don't throw gasoline on it. When the angry person is spewing out words and you engage in argument with him, it is like throwing gasoline on the fire. An angry person can burn all night if you continue to throw gasoline. But when you listen as the anger burns, eventually the fuel of his anger will burn out. When he senses that he has been genuinely heard, he will become open for your help. But until he has been heard, his anger will continue to burn.

This principle also applies to our response to our children. We may be bigger and more powerful, but trying to dominate will not work. Paul admonished fathers to "provoke not your children to wrath" (Ephesians 6:4 KJV). Responding angrily and harshly to a child who is trying to express her anger simply provokes more anger. And a key proverb advises, "A gentle answer turns away wrath, but a harsh word stirs up anger" (Proverbs 15:1). Whether the person is age seven or thirty-seven, harsh words thrown in the face of an angry person will simply stimulate more anger. In contrast, an open heart that listens sympathetically and gives a gentle answer will cause anger to subside. This is the Christian model to which we aspire.

Angry people need someone who cares enough to listen long enough to understand the pain. They need someone who listens carefully enough to identify with the person's anger, wisely enough to express understanding, and courageously enough to respond with a gentle, truthful answer—an answer that seeks resolution of the issue that gave rise to the anger. That is our goal, to help the angry person have a healthy response and a constructive solution.

HOW TO RESPOND TO AN ANGRY PERSON

*T*he following seven steps in responding to an angry person will help calm the individual, keep you calm, and bring the understanding necessary to help the person deal with his anger in a healthy manner.

First, listen to the person. The best thing you can do for an angry person is to listen to his story. As you listen, you're becoming aware of the extent of his anger, and you are getting some basics of the person's story.

Second, listen to the person. Having heard his story, ask the angry person to repeat it. By doing this, you let the angry person know you are taking him seriously, that you really want to understand what happened. The person also senses that you are not condemning his anger.

Third, listen to the person. After listening a second time, now ask additional questions to clarify the situation. It takes at least three rounds of listening, sometimes four, for the angry person to get out all of his or her concerns.

Fourth, seek to understand the angry person's plight. As you try to understand what stimulated the person's anger, ask yourself, "Would I be angry in the same situation?" Try to identify with the person by visualizing yourself having experienced what that person has experienced.

Fifth, express to the person your understanding of the situation. Your statement of understanding should be compassionate and spoken with empathy. Even if the person has some facts wrong, do not try to modify or challenge now; that can come later. Rather, affirm the person's feelings of anger.

Sixth, share additional information that may shed light on the subject. When you present such information at this point, you will not offend; you help the other person to let his anger subside and perhaps to realize that you have not wronged him.

Seventh, confess any wrongdoing and perform restitution. If you realize that the angry person's anger is definitive; that is, you have wronged him, then it is time for your confession and efforts to make right the wrong you have committed.

FOR DISCUSSION

1. In order to avoid the harmful affects of destructive anger, we must be skilled at handling anger in others. Times will come when we encounter other angry people: It may be anger directed against us personally, against institutions we represent, or random anger that arbitrarily falls upon us. Recall a recent experience of anger directed at you by another person. How did you handle it? What was the source of their anger? Was the situation resolved amicably for both parties?

2. The first three crucial steps to handling another person's anger are (1) listen, (2) listen, and (3) listen. This may sound simplistic, but the best way to get at the heart of another person's anger is to listen to him first. In this way, you can best understand what is troubling the person and help him understand and begin to process his own anger. Try a listening exercise. Recount a recent event where you became angry at some institution for some injustice or oversight (this might be a bill which overcharged you for something or a defective product you purchased and tried to return to the store). Then have group members try to assist you in recalling the most important issues and in identifying the source of your anger. Assess how well the group as a whole listened.

3. Besides seeking to understand the angry person's plight, you must attempt to shed additional light on the issue where possible. This will help to focus the person's anger and channel it toward a positive resolution. If a neighbor is angry at you for not being invited to a neighborhood party starting in an hour, you might explain to him that you had handed the invitation to his teenage son a week ago. While this won't help restore the sense of wrong altogether, it now tells the neighbor that you were thinking of him and that there is another explanation for his not receiving an invitation. He must now talk with his son for further resolution. Discuss within the group how you might assist your neighbor in this scenario to come to complete resolution. (For instance, what should your demeanor be like? Should you help in talking with the neighbor's son to prevent a further escalation of tensions?)

4. *Processing your anger:* You are a postal worker in a neighborhood post office. An angry customer approaches you at your counter to complain that for the last week her mail has consistently been confused with other resi-

dent's mail and that she has been picking up her mail from people as far away as two miles. The customer fears that she has not received her federal income tax return check which the IRS claims to have mailed a week ago. The woman is extremely angry and is threatening legal action, naming you and your office if she doesn't receive her check immediately. How do you resolve this anger situation?

Epilogue

GOD'S NATURE IN US

*E*arly in this book, we established the reality that God is both holy and loving. These are two of the fundamental qualities of God's nature. Since we are made in God's image, it should not be surprising to read the words of Peter, "As obedient children, do not conform to the evil desires you had when you lived in ignorance. But just as he who called you is holy, so be holy in all you do; for it is written: 'Be holy, because I am holy'" (1 Peter 1:14–16). Or the words of Jesus, "As I have loved you, so you must love one another" (John 13:34). It is clearly God's desire that His nature be reflected in us.

Learning to understand and process anger in a biblical way is an essential step in Christian discipleship. Perhaps that seems an extreme statement, but it is true. Processing our anger in a biblical way is part of being a follower of Christ. Christians who fail to handle anger responsibly cannot reflect the holiness or the love of God; that is to say, mismanaged anger is far from being holy and far from being loving. Anger is God's gift to man and when handled biblically demonstrates both a reverence for God's holiness and a commitment to loving people. When anger is processed properly, relationships are restored, wrongs are righted, and the world is a better place in which to live. We can sleep at night with a clear conscience, and the people around us can live without fear.

A man or woman who learns to control anger responsibly has taken a giant step in Christian maturity.

I am fully aware that proper anger management is not a lesson learned once and for all. It is a lesson that must be practiced every time we experience anger. When we fail and in our anger sin, we must learn to confess immediately to God and to the person we have sinned against. The biblical admonition is clear—this must be done quickly and thoroughly. (See Ephesians 4:26.) We can and should learn to respond to anger in keeping with God's design.

As noted in chapters 1 and 2, a biblical understanding of the origin and purpose of anger is the starting point for learning to manage anger. Remember, your capacity to experience anger is related to the fact that you are made in the image of God; as such, you have a concern for righteousness and fairness. With that in mind, you and I can face anger with a more positive attitude. Furthermore, if we understand that because we are "fallen" creatures some of our anger may be distorted—that is, it grows out of our self-centered fallen natures rather than a true concern for righteousness—we can better sort through our angry feelings to determine their validity. Remember also that the true purpose of valid anger is to motivate you to take constructive action—to seek to right the wrong. That truth should call you to regularly evaluate your behavior to see if it serves a positive purpose.

Thus, learning to manage your anger becomes a part of your growth into greater Christlikeness. No Christian is spiritually mature who has not learned to evaluate and manage anger in a constructive manner.

Much of the dysfunction in contemporary Christian families is rooted in misunderstood and mismanaged anger. Few tasks in the area of marriage and family life are more important than correcting this widespread anger mismanagement. My sincere hope is that this book will serve as a catalyst in the Christian community to stimulate discussion, prayer, and eventually a clearer understanding of how to respond to the experience of anger. My desire is that you will not only read this book, but through the discussion questions and reflection you will seek to apply its principles to your own life. If married, I hope you will become a positive model for your spouse and children in how to respond to anger. Please don't preach to them until you are consciously trying to grow in your own anger management skills.

Let me suggest three ways you can apply this message in your life and the lives of others:

1. Share this book and its principles with your friends.
2. Suggest the book and the accompanying discussion questions as a study topic for your adult discipleship group. Few topics are more pertinent to marriage and family—and all other human relationships—than the topic of anger.
3. Look for ways to help your non-Christian friends. Classes or conversations focused on proper anger management may be a bridge to a world who has lost its way and is increasingly driven by uncontrolled anger.

If Christians can learn to handle their own anger positively, perhaps God will give us the opportunity to share with our non-Christian friends. If we are not successful in dealing with our own anger, we may find ourselves "losing our cool" with our secular neighbors and thus confirming their suspicion that our Christianity is only skin deep.

In reality, our anger is at the very heart of who we are. Tell me what you are angry about and I will tell you what is important to you. For the mature Christian, anger will focus on true injustice, unfairness, inequity, and ungodliness; not on petty personal irritations. For the mature Christian such anger will motivate positive efforts to establish justice, fairness, equity, and godliness. His anger will be tempered with mercy and humility realizing that he too is capable of falling. To use the words of the ancient Hebrew prophet: "He has showed you, O man, what is good. And what does the Lord require of you? To act justly and to love mercy and to walk humbly with your God" (Micah 6:8).

Such a lofty lifestyle—practicing justice, mercy, and humility in our daily actions—requires first that we reconcile with God through Christ; that gives us the motivation to aspire. Second, it requires the daily empowering work of the Holy Spirit, which enables us to succeed.

Of all peoples, the Christian has the greatest potential for understanding and processing anger to the glory of God. That is the message and goal of this book.

I'm feeling angry right now but don't worry. I'm not going to attack you. But I do need your help.

Is this a good time to talk?

VERSES TO MEMORIZE

"A fool gives full vent to his anger, but a wise man keeps himself under control." (Proverbs 29:11)

"An angry man stirs up dissension, and a hot-tempered one commits many sins." (Proverbs 29:22)

"A quick-tempered man does foolish things." (Proverbs 14:17)

"A patient man has great understanding, but a quick-tempered man displays folly." (Proverbs 14:29)

"In your anger do not sin: Do not let the sun go down while you are still angry, and do not give the devil a foothold." (Ephesians 4:26-27)

FIVE STEPS TO HANDLE VALID ANGER

1. Consciously acknowledge to yourself that you are angry.
2. Restrain your immediate response.
3. Locate the focus of your anger.
4. Analyze your options.
5. Take constructive action.